Curiosities Series

Boston CURIOSITIES

Quirky characters, roadside oddities & other offbeat stuff

Bruce Gellerman and Erik Sherman

Guilford, Connecticut

For my mother and father.
–B. G.

For whatever mad whim first convinced me
to move to the area sight unseen.
–E. S.

To buy books in quantity for corporate use
or incentives, call **(800) 962–0973**
or e-mail **premiums@GlobePequot.com.**

Copyright © 2010 by Morris Book Publishing, LLC

Photos by Bruce Gellerman and Erik Sherman unless otherwise noted

Map by Daniel Lloyd © Morris Book Publishing, LLC

Text design: Bret Kerr

Layout artist: Casey Shain

Project editor: John Burbidge

Library of Congress Cataloging-in-Publication data is available on file.

ISBN 978-0-7627-4841-9

Printed in the United States of America

10 9 8 7 6 5 4 3 2 1

The prices, rates, and hours listed in this guidebook were confirmed at press time. We recommend, however, that you call establishments to obtain current information before traveling.

contents

★ ★

Boston Overview

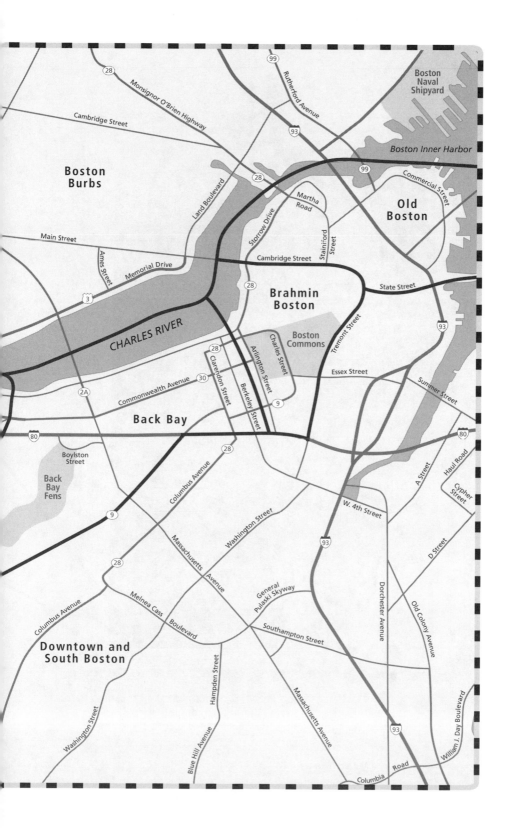

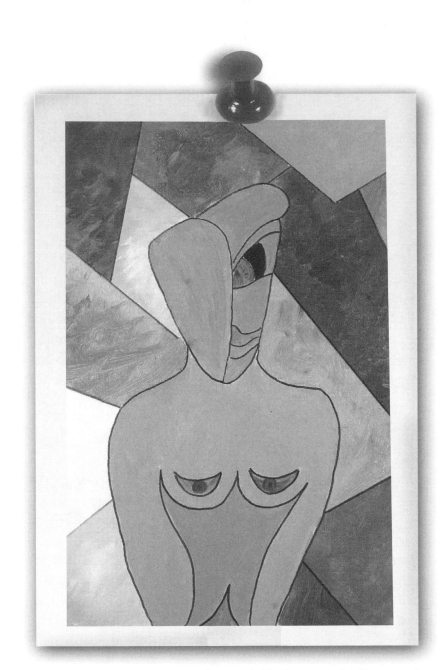

The post-Cubist image at the Museum of Bad Art in Somerville compels the viewer to make direct eye contact.

introduction

★ ★

Boston is a quirky, curious, sort of city. In most places east is east, and west is west. Not so in Boston. The geographical center of present-day Boston is Roxbury, but due north of the center is the South End, which is different than South Boston, which is east of the South End. North of South Boston is East Boston, and southwest of East Boston is the North End. Thankfully, the West End is west of the North End, but you won't find it anymore; most of the community came to an end during the 1950s' rush to urban renewal. Don't even think of orienting yourself using the Old South Church: It's north of the New Old South Church. Confused? Head to the intersection of Summer and Winter Streets, where you'll find a plaque marking the Center of the Universe. It's on the floor of the fruit stand on the corner.

Welcome to Boston! Pass the bananas.

Boston has had centuries to hone its eccentricities. The peninsula was first settled by the Puritans, who left Europe to escape religious persecution and then set up gallows in and around Boston Common to hang those with different religious beliefs. The Puritans purchased the land that was to become Boston from a reclusive Anglican minister who was fond of riding around Beacon Hill naked on a white bull. The Puritans made him a member of their church—against his will. No, you didn't fool with Puritans. They were so strict they even banned Christmas.

But even the Puritans couldn't sour people on Boston, which quickly grew to become the most populated place in the colonies. Perhaps it grew too quickly. In the Old Granary Burying Ground, there are 2,345 gravestones, but an estimated 5,000 people are buried there. One of its most famous permanent residents is John Hancock, whose bold signature on the *Declaration of Independence* taunted the British. Alas, Hancock's name-signing hand is not buried with him. It was stolen by grave robbers soon after he was interred. The Old Granary also has the mortal remains of Sam Adams, Paul Revere, and victims of the Boston Massacre. Near dead center is the largest monument in the cemetery. The 25-foot-tall obelisk marked Franklin doesn't grace the grave of Ben, one of the city's most celebrated native-born citizens, but his parents. Maybe there wasn't room for old Ben. Out of seventeen Franklin children, he was number fifteen.

Times change, but not the city's idiosyncrasies. When the John Hancock Tower was being built in modern Boston, the windows kept popping out, raining shards upon unsuspecting citizens on the street. The building was a real pain in the glass. But don't worry; today when you look up at the Hancock, you'll see beautiful Copley Square and the nearby shopping complex known as the Elephant in Pajamas reflected in the tower's facade. And you don't have to look down either. It's only an elephant figuratively speaking.

Boston's contradictions, quirky streets, and curious history make it one of the world's great walking cities. Our recommendation: Bring a sense of humor, wear a good pair of shoes, and forget the map. It won't help much anyhow. Welcome to Boston.

CHAPTER

1

Old Boston

Walking through some of the oldest parts of Boston—including Faneuil Hall, Government Center, the North End, East Boston, the West End, and Charlestown—you might find yourself looking around for something to overthrow. The seeds of revolution, and a few other things, run deep here. Of course, that doesn't mean some facts don't get twisted around. For example, the monument to the Battle of Bunker Hill isn't on a hill that isn't Bunker Hill. You could brew tea for two thousand of your closest friends or stand where the Boston Massacre took place, that is, if you can dodge the cars driving through. Better than dodging the bull that William Blackstone (also spelled Blaxton, just to make things more confusing), the first Englishman to live in Boston, would ride while in the buff. Want to see the world's ugliest building? It's here. So is a house that Paul Revere owned, restored in a way that would make it completely unrecognizable to him. And there's a plaque to the first man to achieve flight . . . only to have the town fathers ban the activity. Maybe one of them had a real-estate interest in Kitty Hawk.

★ ★

The Ice King Cometh
Charlestown

Some titans of industry have ice water running in their veins, but none more than Frederic Tudor, the Ice King. In the early nineteenth century, if you wanted something cold to drink on a hot day, you were simply out of luck, particularly if you lived in a hot part of the world, like the Caribbean or New Orleans, and had no winter sources of lake ice, let alone icehouses to store slabs. Tudor knew a market when he saw one and moved quickly to freeze out his potential competition. His first attempts ended up as so many puddles, but undaunted, and with help from his friend Nathaniel Wyeth, an ancestor of the artist Andrew Wyeth, Tudor developed new ways to insulate and ship ice, as well as a plow to cut uniform blocks. He eventually would ship ice from Walden Pond and Fresh Pond, sending it by train to Tudor's Wharf in Charlestown. The ice business shifted from there to the freezer in your own home, but the wharf still stands next to the USS *Constitution* in the Charlestown Navy Yard.

Making the Rounds
Charlestown

A winning season is a notable feat, particularly in Boston, where the sports teams have known fate's capriciousness. But although it took three tries to launch the USS *Constitution,* the oldest commissioned naval ship afloat today, it never lost a battle at sea. It could take on any vessel its size and could outrun bigger ones, as its top speed was 13 knots with all thirty-six sails rigged. Its nickname, Old Ironsides, comes from the hull construction, unusually thick and heavily braced for the time, and the use of a particularly dense and tough wood called southern live oak. In a famous battle with the HMS *Guerriere* during the War of 1812, cannonballs seemed to bounce off its sides. The *Constitution* was retired from active service in 1881 but continues to participate in special events and travels out to Castle Island several times a year. When it does, there is a ticket lottery for a chance to be on deck for the trip. To catch the *Constitution* when it's not moving, go to 1 Constitution Road. You can find visitor hours and other information at www.ussconstitution.navy.mil/.

Battle of ... Where Did You Say?
Charlestown

The Bunker Hill Monument is austere and tall—221 feet, with 294 stairs inside that lead to the top and a marvelous view at the end of the climb. The order of Colonel William Prescott, not to shoot until the colonists could see the whites of the British troops' eyes, has become a legend studied by generations of American schoolchildren. Too bad that the battle it commemorates actually took place elsewhere.

This first major battle of the American Revolution happened early, in June 1775, during the Siege of Boston. New England militias under the command of George Washington had surrounded the city, trying to keep the British troops there unable to deploy. After a couple of months of this, the British decided to try and occupy hills around Boston to get leverage and open a route out of the city. Prescott took 1,200 militiamen to occupy both Bunker Hill and Breed's Hill, a lower spot. The ill-trained colonists repelled two waves of attacks by 5,000 British, causing heavy casualties among the British. Running out of ammunition, they had to retreat on the third attack. The British won, but with 226 killed and 800 wounded, it was a stinging experience and showed that the largely untrained militias could fight. Although the colonists did retreat over Bunker Hill, the bulk of the fighting happened on Breed's Hill because it was closer to Boston and more easily defended. Even though Bunker Hill got the publicity, the monument itself is actually on Breed's Hill in Monument Square.

Vintage Tavern
Charlestown

In colonial times, taverns were important establishments, serving food and drink, and a place where movers and shakers could meet. The

★ ★

oldest tavern in Massachusetts still in operation is the Warren Tavern in Charlestown, built in 1780—likely the first building erected after the British razed the town following the Battle of Bunker Hill (or Battle of Breed's Hill to aficionados) and named for an American hero of that fight and a major force in the early days of the revolution. Paul Revere was a frequent patron, and George Washington drank (but didn't sleep) there. If you feel the urge to hoist a pint in memory of those who went before, you'll find the Warren on 2 Pleasant Street. Call (617) 241-8142 or visit www.warrentavern.com.

First Women of Medicine
Charlestown

Professional life was difficult for women involved in medicine in the nineteenth century, but you can remember two pioneer female physicians who both happened to have worked in Charlestown. Harriot Kezia Hunt was an early American practicing physician, although her first twenty years of professional life were without a degree. She was the first woman who applied to the Harvard Medical School (twice, though she was turned down both times because the male students refused to be around a woman) and may have been the first American woman to work professionally as a physician. She founded a women's physiological society in Charlestown.

Rebecca Lee Crumpler was the first African-American woman to receive a medical degree in the United States. She matriculated from the New England Female Medical College in 1864. (The school would merge with Boston University nine years later.) She and her husband would eventually live for a while at 67 Joy Street in Beacon Hill. But before becoming a doctor and working with the black community, she was a nurse for eight years in Charlestown.

You can remember both of them at the MGH Charlestown Health-Care Center at 73 High Street.

Old City Hall: First, Second, and Last in Boston History
Downtown

The cornerstone of Old City Hall was laid on December 22, 1862, the anniversary of the landing of the Pilgrims at Plymouth. It is built on the site of the city's first two city halls and is an example of the French Second Empire architectural style, one of the first to be built in the United States and one of the last surviving examples of the style.

Two-time Boston mayor Joseph Wightman, the first Democratic Party member to hold the position, dedicated the building. Inside the cornerstone is a 15-by-15-by-6-inch copper box, surrounded by pulverized charcoal, containing another 13-by-13-by-4-inch copper box that holds a number of historic mementos, including a map of the city; the *Boston Almanac*; the *Annual Report of the Chief of Police*;

Boston's Old City Hall is an example of the French Second Empire architectural style.

★ ★

and a sealed glass bottle with $1 and $2 U.S. Treasury notes, postal currency, and a $20 Treasury note from the "Confederate States of America."

Mayor Wightman had fought hard to deliver humanitarian aid to Confederate POWs imprisoned in Fort Warren in Boston Harbor and was a leader in providing financial aid to Union soldiers and their families. Fifteen years after laying the cornerstone, Mayor Wightman himself was imprisoned in Boston for not paying a debt it was later determined he did not owe. If you can break out of where you are, the Old City Hall is at 45 School Street. Call (617) 523-8678 or visit www.oldcityhall.com.

Tea for Two . . . Thousand
Faneuil Hall

It is only right and proper that the city where the most famous tea party in history took place would have the world's largest teakettle. The Oriental Teashop had the giant pot cast in 1873 and hung in September 1874. To promote the tea shop, the company held a

Lobsta Mickey

Mickey Mouse was born November 18, 1928. That was the day *Steamboat Willie* hit the silver screen, becoming the first synchronized sound cartoon. Here in Boston's Faneuil Hall Market-place, Mickey would be best if he *were* steamed. The 700-pound statue of *Lobsta Mickey* was created by artist Breanna Rowlette in 2003. It's one of seventy-five unique Mickeys commissioned by The Walt Disney Company to commemorate the world's most famous movie mouse. Pass the butter.

Tea for two . . . two thousand, that is. The
giant teapot in Boston's City Hall Plaza has been
spouting steam since 1873.

contest on New Year's Day in 1875. The public was invited to guess
the capacity of the giant kettle. Twelve thousand people cast ballots.
As officials began to pour cups into the kettle, a boy popped out,
then another, and another. Finally, eight boys emerged, followed by
a 6-foot man—the designer of the kettle. The winner got a 40-pound
chest of tea. You'll find the exact capacity engraved on the side of

★ ★

the kettle: precisely 227 gallons, 2 quarts, 1 pint, and 3 gills. The giant kettle was moved from its original location, not far from here, in 1967. Ironically, the kettle now hangs above a Starbucks store at 63 Court Street near the Government Center metro station. Perhaps if the java chain had been around in 1770, we might be calling it the "Boston Coffee Klatch" today.

First in War
Faneuil Hall

The Ancient and Honorable Artillery Company of Massachusetts is no newcomer. Organized in 1637 and chartered by Governor John Winthrop in 1638, this is the first official military company in the Western Hemisphere. Since then, the group has been in existence, holding annual elections for officers on the Boston Common each June. This company was a busy one, and not just in military matters. As its Web site notes, "The members of the Company trod the fields of every battlefield of New England; they fought for freedom on foreign soil; they judged the courts; they pleaded at the bar; they instituted town government and leveled forests; and they were active in settling the towns of the frontier." U.S. presidents James Monroe, Chester A. Arthur, Calvin Coolidge, and John F. Kennedy all belonged, and over the decades, eight members won the Medal of Honor. The headquarters and a museum open to the public on weekdays are on the fourth floor of Faneuil Hall. You can read more about the tradition of the Company at www.ahac.us.com/history.htm.

The Real Boston Massacre
Faneuil Hall

The site of the Boston Massacre marks the spot where British troops killed five colonists on the evening of March 5, 1770. Tensions were running high as colonists became increasingly angry over the imposition of new taxes. A crowd of 300 to 400 gathered in front of the

Old State House. No one knows who fired the first shots, and it may have started as a misunderstanding. A church bell, used as a signal for fire, rang out. Someone yelled "Fire," and bullets began to fly.

While the site of the Boston Tea Party is still disputed, the precise location of the Boston Massacre is known. It's at the intersection of Devonshire and State Streets. A circle of cobblestones, in the middle of the intersection, marks the site. Be careful: Boston drivers can still cause a massacre.

The site of the Boston Massacre marks the spot where
British troops killed five colonists.

Big Shoes to Fill

Faneuil Hall

There are a few names synonymous with basketball in Boston, and
none more widely known than Larry Bird. Number 33 was with the
Celtics from 1979 to 1992 and earned his place in the Basketball
Hall of Fame as a three-time Most Valuable Player, twelve-time NBA
Eastern Conference All-Star, and gold medal Olympian. His value as a
player came more from his incessantly hard work than from an abun-
dance of natural ability. He was a great high school player, continued
after some struggles into college, and eventually joined the Celtics
after his senior year. When he finally retired as a player because
of injuries and back problems, he could look back at averaging 24
points, 10 rebounds, and 6 assists per game. The Celtics retired his

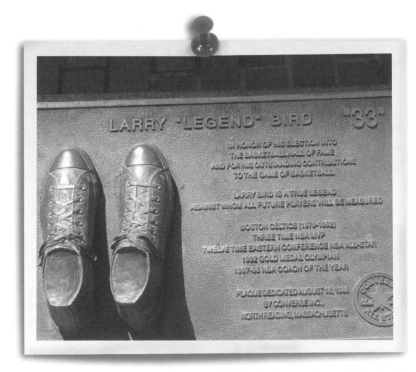

Big Bird's shoes—Larry Bird, that is.

number when he left. He was a big man: 6 foot, 9 inches and 220 pounds when drafted, with a size 13 shoe. He's no longer in Boston, but a bronzed pair of his shoes is, as part of a plaque in Faneuil Hall Marketplace, next to the statue of legendary Celtics coach Red Auerbach.

Americans "In-vest" in an Insect
Faneuil Hall

Since 1742, a 52-inch-tall, 38-pound copper grasshopper with glass doorknob eyes has looked down onto a good deal of American history. The 'hopper has watched from his weather vane perch 80 feet above the ground as the winds of change turned the colonies into a nation and the nation into a world superpower. From the grasshopper's vantage point atop Faneuil Hall, the insect has been an eyewitness to the Boston Massacre and the Boston Tea Party and watched as patriotic conspirators gathered at the Old Meeting House. Over time the grasshopper has survived wars, hurricanes, earthquakes, fires, and vandals.

But the grasshopper is more than a priceless piece of Americana. It is also a time capsule. Inside the insect's stomach is a copper container. Each time the grasshopper has been handled and restored, people have placed objects into the vane and taken things out.

In 1761, following a devastating fire and an earthquake, a note inscribed "Food for the Grasshopper" was inserted into the copper time capsule by the restorer. The note, detailing the gilded insect's trials and tribulations, is now in the Boston Public Library's archives.

The weather vane was restored again in 1842. This time it was filled with papers and coins. It is believed that the first contents were removed and sold at auction in 1885. In 1889 some newspapers and coins from the period were deposited in the capsule, and in 1952 Boston's mayor added one of his business cards and a message.

In 1974 the grasshopper was reported missing, and a massive insect hunt was started.

The grasshopper time capsule is perched 80 feet
above the ground on Faneuil Hall.

The 'hopper was discovered weeks later in the Faneuil Hall belfry
underneath a pile of old flags. Seems painters had taken it down and
forgot to put it back up. A tip from an ex-steeplejack who worked on
the vane and was trying to beat a drug rap led to its recovery. Before
the grasshopper was restored to its proper perch, Boston's mayor
resealed all of the items in the capsule, adding a letter of his own and
two bicentennial coins.

JFK Ate Here

Faneuil Hall

Obviously, John F. Kennedy ate at a lot of places in his hometown.
One of his favorites was the Union Oyster House, where the Kennedy clan dined regularly on the restaurant's namesake mollusk. In

the private upstairs dining room, you will find a plaque on Kennedy's favorite booth, number 18, dedicated to his memory in 1977. Kennedy was just one of many Harvard students to frequent the restaurant. Supposedly, some were paid to eat there. Oyster House lore has it that an importer of toothpicks from South America hired Harvard students to dine at the restaurant and request the picks as a way to boost sales. The Union Oyster House is located at 41 Union Street. To request a table or JFK's favorite booth, call (617) 227-2750 or visit www.unionoysterhouse.com.

High Watermark
Faneuil Hall

When Boston was founded, a walk about town was more likely a slosh. Much of the city is built on what was formerly marsh, with landfill used to provide save travel. Actually, landfill is a euphemism, as the Atlantic used to be the city's dump, whether regular waste or the remains of the frequent fires. When enough debris accumulated, Boston would cover it over with dirt and build right on top of it.

That brings us to Faneuil Hall. Things are more or less high and dry now, minus the stray spilled tourist drink. But when the building was constructed in 1742, a gift of wealthy city resident Peter Faneuil a year before his death, it was actually at the water's edge. This was Boston's first marketplace, and having easy access to vessels made sense. Eventually, the original hall burned down in 1761, was rebuilt a year later, and became a home to stirring speeches in support of independence from Britain. (In fact, until the 1900s, it was the main location for local political debate.) In the early nineteenth century, the architect of the State House, Charles Bulfinch, created a plan to use the walls of the structure while redesigning it to be twice the height and width. But to get a sense of what things were like in Boston all those years ago, enter the hall, walk to the end, and gaze out the doors, imagining the ocean within steps.

With Your Clothes on, I See the Resemblance
Faneuil Hall

It's only fitting that in a town known for its quirky characters, the first Englishman to call Boston home was an eccentric, hermit bookworm who enjoyed romping on Beacon Hill astride his white bull while in the buff. William Blackstone (aka Blaxston), an Anglican minister, set up home and library on Beacon Hill in 1625. Five years later, in an act of Christian charity, the reclusive Blackstone invited John Winthrop and his band of Puritan settlers to join him and share his freshwater spring. The Puritans had originally settled in nearby Charlestown but lacked clean water and were dying of disease.

The Founders' Monument, in Boston Common, commemorates the 300th anniversary of Blackstone's welcoming Winthrop and the

Founders' Monument is located in Boston Common, across from Spruce and Beacon Streets.

Puritans. Native Americans who called the place Shawmut can also be seen in the bas-relief sculpture by John Paramino. In the foreground is Blackstone's spring. The monument was dedicated during James Michael Curley's second term as Boston's mayor. Curley, known as the Rascal King, served four terms as mayor, once as governor and once in federal prison for mail fraud.

You'll notice that Blackstone, who liked to go bare butt on Beacon Hill, is fully clothed in the monument. But look closely. You'll notice Blackstone bears a striking resemblance to Mayor Curley. Sculptor Paramino used a contemporary painting of John Winthrop to guide him in creating the Puritan's likeness, but no such image existed for Blackstone. In a politically astute move, Paramino cast Curley as the model. You'll find two statues of Hizzonah, the mayor, in tiny Union Park near Faneuil Hall. In one, Curley is standing; in the other, he's sitting. In both, he's wearing clothes.

Infrequent Flier

Boston's Logan International Airport, one of the busiest in the nation, is named in honor of Lieutenant General Edward Lawrence Logan. Logan was born in Boston in 1875 and led a distinguished career as an elected official, judge, and war hero. He died in 1929.

The question is, Why did city officials name an airport after him? After all, for all of his many accomplishments, Lieutenant General Logan never flew in an airplane.

★ ★

Lady Madonna
East Boston

Not far from Suffolk Downs Racetrack and overlooking Logan International Airport is the Madonna, Queen of the Universe National Shrine. The 35-foot bronze-and-copper statue was created by Italian-Jewish sculptor Arrigo Minerbi and set on the site in 1954.

Driving up the winding road to the shrine, you will see a 50-foot cross atop a hill. The hill is where the second battle of the American Revolution was fought. The views of Boston and the airport from the top of the hill are terrific. A gift shop near the shrine offers unusual religious objects for sale. The Madonna, Queen of the Universe National Shrine is at 111 Orient Avenue, East Boston. (617) 569-2100. Follow the signs on Route 1A.

World's Ugliest Building
Government Center

How times and tastes have changed! When Boston's City Hall was finished in 1969, a poll, conducted by the American Institute of Architects, voted it the sixth greatest building in America. In 2008 readers and editors of the travel Web site www.Virtualtourist.com named it "the world's ugliest building."

The nine-story inverted pyramid, constructed of raw precast concrete and brick, is a stunning example of the 1960s' Brutalist style. Architects Gerhard Kallmann and Noel Michael McKinnell won a national competition for their design. The committee that selected the plan called it "a keystone between the historic past and the brilliant future which is to come." Today, many Bostonians would like to make it part of the city's past and reduce it to rubble. One critic described it as "the crate Faneuil Hall came in."

After Mayor Thomas Menino announced in 2007 that he wanted to tear down the building, the city's Landmarks Commission was presented with a petition that would grant the building landmark status and prevent its destruction.

★ ★

Clearly, beauty is in the eye of the beholder, but there's no dispute that Boston's City Hall is ugly to the bone. It's cold and drafty, the roof leaks, and one city council member says, even after working in it for three years, he still gets lost in the baffling maze on the top floor.

Perhaps critics would have been kinder if the European-born architects' original vision had been realized. They initially wanted the building to have a beer hall in the basement.

The surrounding eight-acre plaza is also considered an abysmal failure of design and urban planning. In 2004 the Project for Public Spaces identified it as the worst single public plaza worldwide. There were hundreds of contenders.

The world's ugliest building.

Oy, You Should Only Live So Long and Prosper!

Mr. Spock from the TV series *Star Trek* comes from Vulcan via Boston. Leonard Nimoy, aka Spock, grew up in an Orthodox Jewish household in Boston's West End. His religious background played a pivotal role in developing his Vulcan character.

According to Nimoy, the idea for the Vulcan salute, with four fingers of each hand split, comes from a boyhood lesson he learned at temple. The gesture creates the Hebrew letter *shin,* representing the first letter of the Almighty and the word *peace.* Nimoy proposed the hand signal when the producers of the show were trying to come up with a salute for his character.

After *Star Trek* went into syndication, Nimoy became a world-renowned photographer, returning to the art he learned when he was of bar mitzvah age. Using the family camera, he took photos of friends and family members,

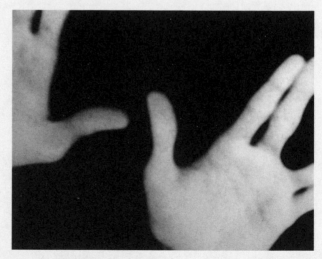

This photograph of the Vulcan/shin salute is part of Nimoy's "The Hand Series."
Courtesy of Leonard Nimoy and R. Michelson Galleries, Northampton, Massachusetts

developing the shots in the bathroom of his family's Boston apartment. Check out Nimoy's photos on his Web page (www.leonardnimoy photography.com). The pointy-eared Vulcan's out-of-this world haircut might also be explained: His father was a barber.

A Slice of Boston History

Government Center

The narrow walkway connecting City Hall Avenue and Washington Street is known as Pi Alley. At least, that's the way it's spelled on Google Maps. The Street Department of the City of Boston lists it as Pie Street. You decide.

Over the centuries the alley was home to a succession of businesses. There was Gridley Restaurant, then Thompson's Spa, George Bray's Bakery, and later Henry's Hole in the Wall. All sold pie. Henry's was famous for its meat-filled slices known as "Cat Pie."

That was long before the 1900s, when nearby Washington Street became known as Newspaper Row, home to eight daily Boston newspapers. As the story goes, newspaper typesetters would carry loose pieces of lead type known as "pi" in their pockets and dump them in the alley as they walked to the Bell in Hand tavern after work. Pie or Pi: It's not so easy.

Pi/Pie Alley connects Washington and City Hall Avenue between School and Court Streets.

Queen of the Tassel Tossers

Government Center

Sally Keith had a love-hate affair with tassels. The day she saw one on the end of a window shade, she was inspired to use them in her strip tease show. Sally Keith was "Queen of the Tassel Tossers" on Boston's Crawford House vaudeville stage. From the 1930s to 1950s, she reigned supreme, tossing tassels like no other. Sally, whose real name was Sylvia, mounted them on her breasts and made them spin in opposite directions. They spun fast and furiously like airplane propellers. Then things really took off. The platinum blonde would turn around and begin tossing tassels on her tush, swinging them independently as if they had minds of their own.

Sally Keith was "Queen of the Tassel Tossers" on Boston's Crawford House vaudeville stage.

Sailors shipping out of Boston during World War II proved to be loyal Sally fans. So were local businessmen and students. She told the *Harvard Crimson* newspaper, "I hate my tassels, but the boys love them." She said she could always spot a Harvard man in the crowd: "Harvardians know a good thing when they see it, and I do try to let them see it." One Harvard professor of medicine brought his students to the theater to learn which muscles Sally used to twirl her tatas.

Women also loved Sally's show. One female patron once said," I would have made a million bucks in the ladies' room at the Crawford House. During intermission I'd go in to powder my nose, and I'd see all the women standing in front of the mirror trying to make themselves go in opposite directions."

Sally also had a big heart. One of Boston Mayor Curley's sons was a priest at a North End parish and recalls the day Sally offered to donate a pair of tassels to a church fund-raising raffle. The good father turned down the generous gift.

Crawford House burned down in 1948, and the area known as Scollay Square, where Sally Keith once reigned supreme, was demolished in 1962 to make way for Government Center.

Local historian David Kruh wrote the definitive history of Sally Keith in his books *Always Something Doing* and *Scollay Square.* For more information, check out his Web site: www.joeandnemo.com.

Strip Search

Government Center

Boston has an interesting historic double existence as determined saint and riotous sinner. This is the land of banned books and political riots, of enforced religious observance and revolutionary intent, of blue blood and blue laws. Part of the more checkered past was the old Howard Athenaeum, otherwise known as the Old Howard, a famous theater that eventually would become home to burlesque in Boston. Its history incorporates that intersection of high and low. It was originally created in 1844 as a meeting place for a religious group that believed in the imminent end of the world. Guess what? The end didn't happen, and some of the congregation decided to make up their investment losses by selling the building to a theatrical promoter. Four years of Shakespeare and drawing room comedies later, the building burned down but was rebuilt in granite. Again it housed theater, ballet, and some of the great theatrical names, including Sarah Bernhardt and various members of the Booth dynasty. (John Wilkes played Hamlet at the Howard the year before playing assassin at Ford's Theatre in Washington, D.C.)

As immigrants moved into the Scollay Square neighborhood, the Brahmins (a term coined by Oliver Wendell Holmes Sr. in an 1860 article referring to upper-crust New England families) moved out, and everything changed. In 1868 the Old Howard started to advertise vaudeville and burlesque shows, with variety acts and, yes, strippers. Thomas Alva Edison wrote in his diary of a trip to the theater and his seat in the "bald-headed section," noting the tradition of seating men with bald pates in the front row. Some performing greats appeared on the stage, including Phil Silvers. The Old Howard closed in 1953 after Boston police filmed a stripper in action. There were attempts to restore the building and put it back into use, but they ended with a fire in 1961. Eventually, the Old Howard was demolished along with the rest of Scollay Square as part of the Government Center "revitalization." But in Government Center there is a plaque in honor of the famous establishment. Go to 2 Center Plaza and head up the escalator.

Revere Where?
North End

If you want to see the oldest building in downtown Boston, then it's time for a trip to Paul Revere's House. The building is on the site of the former parsonage of the Second Church of Boston, home to the famous preacher Increase Mather and his witch-hunting son, Cotton. The Great Fire of 1676 laid waste to the structure, but four years later, a merchant built his home on the same spot. Revere bought the house in 1770 for himself, his wife, their six children, and mother. He sold the house in 1800, and it passed through a number of owners and purposes, including a tenement, a cigar factory, a bank, and a produce shop. A descendant of Revere bought it in 1902 to keep it safe, and six years later it became one of the first house museums in the country.

The irony, though, is that Revere would never recognize the house. Its outside and one room were restored to a late-seventeenth-century

Holding Down the Fort

History recalls the home at 19 North Square in Boston's North End as the Paul Revere House. It should be noted it was also Rachel Revere's home, and she ran it while her husband was yelling and galloping around at night. Revere never made it to Concord on his famous midnight ride in April 1775. He was captured by the British and prohibited from returning to Boston. It left Rachel Walker Revere alone at home. Alone, except for their six children.

Rachel Revere held down the fort while Paul took up residence downriver in Watertown, where he quickly set up a press to print money for the colonies. She ran not only the household but also Revere's many business ventures. Eventually, she joined him in Watertown, returning home after the British evacuated Boston in 1776.

Across the street from the family's home is Rachel Revere Park, which was dedicated in 1946 and restored in time for America's Bicentennial by Massachusetts Charitable Mechanic Association. Its founding president was Paul Revere.

look, with only three other rooms taking an eighteenth-century ambience that would have felt timely to the silversmith. And even if he recognized it, he'd probably want to call attention to the brick house on Charter Street that he bought when he was sixty-five and far more prosperous. That is, if the house still existed, which it doesn't. The site is currently home to the Eliot School, a Boston public elementary school. You can find the Revere House at 19 North Square, or go to www.paulreverehouse.org for more information.

Let Them Eat Sandwiches!
North End

Boston's first public playground was a sandbox. The "sand garden," as it was called in those days, was built in 1886 by the philanthropic women of the North End Union. It was created to serve the needs of immigrant Italian, Irish, and Jewish children in the area.

At the time, Kate Gannett Wells of the philanthropic committee said, "Playing in the dirt is the royalty of childhood." The site at 20 Parmenter Street is across from the North End branch of the Boston Public Library, where you will find a diorama of the ducal palace of Venice made by the local artist Louise Stimson in the 1940s. We don't know if the palace had its own sandbox.

A Clean Getaway, except for the Smell
North End

On January 17, 1950, robbers broke into the Brinks offices in Boston's North End. They made off with $1,218,211.29 in cash and $1,557,183.83 in securities and checks. The Great Brinks Robbery was the biggest heist in U.S. history. It took six years and $29 million for the government to find and prosecute the crooks. Only $51,906 of the Brinks cash was ever recovered. A big breakthrough in the case came when one of the robbers tried to pass off money that he had hidden in the dirt. The buried loot became smelly and moldy and led to the case being cracked.

Photo by Bruce Gellerman

The building where the famous Brinks job was pulled off made for a speedy getaway: All four floors have direct access to ground level.

The building where thieves pulled off the Great Brinks Robbery still stands and is now known as the North Terminal Garage. It is on the National Register of Historic Places.

The address is 600 Commercial Street.

Is That a Sign, or Are You Just Pleased to See Me?
North End

The basement at 292 Hanover Street has a long history as a den of illicit vices. During Prohibition it was a speakeasy, serving illegal liquor. Today, it is once again a place where people go to engage in sinful behavior: It's a cigar shop, one of the few public places in

★ ★

Boston where it's still legal to smoke. What else would it be with a giant cigar sign hanging outside? Late in 2008, Boston's Public Health Commission voted to ban cigar bars from the city. That ignited a firestorm of protest from smokers, so the commission decided to let things smolder for a while longer. The ban won't go into effect for ten years, and then cigar bars can ask for one more decade-long extension.

So far there's been no proposal to stub out the stogie-holding statue in Faneuil Hall of Boston's beloved Red Auerbach, the coach of the Celtics. You can find Stanza dei Sigari at 292 Hanover Street. Call (617) 227-0295 or visit www.stanzadeisigari.com.

Sometimes a cigar is just a cigar. A big one.

Molasses Mayhem
North End

Although the headline of this entry might be mildly amusing (at least to us), there was nothing funny about the Boston Molasses Flood in 1919. Four years before had seen the construction of a big tank—50 feet tall and 90 feet across—meant to hold molasses, a key ingredient both in rum and in the production of industrial alcohol. Putting a storage tank near the North End made sense, as that kept it close to the water and shipping. However, early on the structure showed signs of leaking. Workers and neighbors complained, but the owner, Purity Distilling Company, did nothing. On January 15, significant temperature changes set off fearsome fermentation, blowing off the top of the tank and throwing huge sheets of steel from the sides of the tank through the air. More than 2 million gallons of molasses swept down the streets in waves reaching anywhere from 8 to 25 feet in height, depending on the account you read. The crushing liquid demolished buildings, killed at least twenty-one people, injured dozens more, killed horses, and stopped traffic with the mix of thick liquid and debris. The disaster led to strengthened safety regulations and the adoption of licensing for construction engineers. You can see the site of the tank and a commemorative marker at 529 Commercial Street.

Cropped Copp's
North End

The North End has the second oldest graveyard in Boston, established in 1660, which is to say, one of the oldest in the country. Its name: Copp's Hill Burying Ground. You'll find a share of famous denizens, including the father and son preaching duo of Increase and Cotton Mather (the latter of Salem witch trial fame) and Edmund Hartt, whose shipyard built the USS *Constitution*.

You might wonder about the name. It doesn't take much time walking through the area to notice that, while there are some hills, this spot is not particularly vertical. Don't feel bad, as even in the late

1800s, younger generations were forgetting that what they saw in Boston wasn't necessarily what their ancestors saw. The land had at least 7 feet lopped off the top to provide dirt so that the city could build a road, now Commercial Street. This was a common practice, resulting in the shearing of other spots, including Beacon Hill, which had originally taken its name from the fires built on the once-existing peak. However, even if the land is squatter than it once was, you can still visit the graveyard at the intersection of Hull and Snow Hill Streets.

A Death-defying Colonial Daredevil

North End

One if by land, two if by sea. Three if by air? Boston's Old North Church, perhaps best known as the place where Paul Revere got the signal that set him off on his midnight ride, also happens to be where colonial stuntman John Childs took the first flight in Boston history. In 1757, eighteen years before Revere got his signal, John Childs used the church steeple as a launching pad. A plaque on a wall outside the Old North Church describes how Childs flew from the 190-foot steeple "to the satisfaction of a great number of spectators."

There are two versions of the event. One has Childs strapping on a leather umbrella-like contraption, putting a grooved wooden board on his chest, and sliding headfirst down a 700-foot-long guy line. The other version has him wearing canvas wings and gliding down. Either way, the colonial daredevil drew such a large crowd that he did it again the next day while shooting off pistols. The performance proved too much for Boston's Puritan prudes. They banned all future flights of fantasy, a prohibition on aviation that stands on the city's books to this day. The plaque commemorating Childs's flight is the third from the left on the brick Washington Garden wall near the main entrance to the Old North Church, 193 Salem Street. Visit www.oldnorth.com for information.

The Skinny House

North End

Ever hear the joke about the hotel room that was so small you had to walk out of it to turn around? That's almost the case for the 135-plus-year-old Skinny House. With a top width of 10 feet, 5 inches, it is the narrowest house in Boston. This house is so skinny

The house at 44 Hull Street in Boston is the skinniest one in the city, and perhaps in the entire commonwealth.

you have to walk down an alley along its side to find a door. At its narrowest, it's under 7 feet. There are a total of five doors in the entire building, even though there are four (OK, three and a half) floors. So, why did anyone design something so … unusual? According to legend, it was for spite. There are a few versions of the story, none definitive, but the general sense is that two people were fighting. One of them had a big house, and the other owned this tiny strip of land. So the second one built the slight domicile to cut off light and air from the big one.

Is it a tall tale? Admittedly, that's a pretty thin story. More likely it is the last of a series of similar homes built in the area around 1800. At one time eleven people lived in the house. Ironically, the Skinny House has a spacious, 1,000-square-foot backyard, one of the largest in the densely populated North End.

The Skinny House is located directly opposite Copp's Hill Burying Ground, at 44 Hull Street. The house number is on the side. Oh, but don't go down the alley or into the backyard. Apparently people have done this and disturbed whoever is holding their breath and living there.

No Bones about It—Cliff Is Back
West End

After 65 million years, Cliff is back. Cliff is a triceratops and just one of five triceratops skeletons ever found. It's considered by many experts the most complete in the world. The bones were dug up in 2004 in North Dakota's Hell Creek formation. Somehow the fossil found its way to an auction in Paris, where an anonymous Boston bidder won the find. As part of the sale, the bidder got naming rights, so he called it "Cliff" after his grandfather.

The distinctive three-horned triceratops were enormous animals. Cliff is 23 feet long from the tip of his tail to his nose, and his skull alone weighs 800 pounds. Curiously, Cliff and his brethren tri-tops were vegetarians, and paleontologists believe their fierce horns were

After sixty-five million years, Cliff is back.

used as much for attracting the opposite sex as fending off their fiendish carnivorous foe, the tyrannosaur (*T. rex* to friends). Assembling Cliff was quite a challenge. It's not like triceratops come with *CliffsNotes*. The Museum of Science is at 1 Science Park. Hours and exhibit times vary, so call (617) 723-2500, or go online to www.mos.org.

Four-Star Jail

West End

Liberty Hotel is the city's newest four-star hotel and one of the nation's oldest jails. It's listed on the state and national Registers of Historic Places. Originally the Charles Street Jail, the granite structure was built in 1851 and designed to house hardened criminals in 220 cells. Among its "guests" were the Boston Strangler, Albert DeSalvo; the anarchists Nicola Sacco and Bartolomeo Vanzetti; Malcolm X; and Mayor James Michael Curley, who served time for cheating on a civil service test. The jail closed under court order in 1990 and reopened after a $150 million makeover in 2007. There are 280 luxury rooms, including one-bedroom "Escape" suites. You can still see vestiges of jail cells in the lobby bar, and one of the restaurants is named Clink. Reportedly, an inmate once escaped to the roof of the jail and held hostages at bay, refusing to release them until they correctly named the members of TV's *Brady Bunch*. Talk about a criminal act. They should have thrown the television, not just the book, at him. You can check into (or out of) the hotel at 215 Charles Street, Beacon Hill (617-224-4000; www.libertyhotel.com).

2

Downtown and South Boston

Stuffy Boston has *its humorous underside. Need a good laugh? Stop by the American Comedy Archives. Near the heart of the financial district you can find the location where a stripper dropping her garb helped bring down a powerful congressman. There's the spot where Alexander Graham Bell didn't invent the telephone, the birthplace of a famous roll, and the site of the original Ponzi scheme. Nowhere else did someone invent the political practice of gerrymandering, and nowhere else can you find the burial plot where they put the remains of John Hancock, minus his famous hand. You can even see the copper plate on which Paul Revere engraved his famous image of the Boston Massacre . . . that he stole from someone else. Hear the birthplace of the science of acoustics and see where the first World Series started and ended. If all of this seems a bit hard to believe, you could take a stop at the world's first central sewage plant.*

Freemasons No Longer Stonewalling
Chinatown

The oldest Freemason lodge in the Western Hemisphere was founded in Boston in 1733. The Most Worshipful Grand Lodge of Free and Accepted Masons of Massachusetts isn't a secret society anymore, but it does still have some hidden historic treasures.

Inside a large vault in the Grand Secretary's office is a small safe. Inside the safe is a revolver. The pistol belonged to the founder of the U.S. Navy, John Paul Jones. He was a Mason. Also in the safe is a velvet-lined box holding two tiny urns, each about the length of an index finger. One urn holds a lock of President James Garfield's hair; he was a Mason. The other holds hair from the father of our country. That's right, old George Washington was also a Mason. They're just two of

Hidden treasures can be found at Boston's Columbian Lodge.

the sixteen U.S. presidents who were members of the fraternal order. So were Paul Revere, Sam Adams, Ben Franklin, and John Hancock, along with the magician Harry Houdini and Mark Twain.

Today, the fraternal order that started as a medieval guild for stoneworkers in Europe has two million members in the United States. But these days the only requirement to become a Mason is to be a man and believe in a supreme being—you don't have to have a clue about how to actually work with stones. Two previous Grand Lodges at this location burned down. The current lodge was dedicated in 1899. The lodge (officially called the Columbian Lodge) is located at 186 Tremont Street, at the corner of Boylston and Tremont Streets. Call (617) 426-6040 for information, or to take a virtual tour visit www.columbianlodge.org.

Leaf Me Liberty
Chinatown

This country's national symbol may be the bald eagle, but during the Revolution, the emblem of Bostonians struggling for independence came from another part of the biological kingdom. The Liberty Tree was a nearly 130-year-old elm that stood at what is today the edge of Chinatown. In 1765 Parliament levied the Stamp Act, which required a variety of documents to carry a tax stamp. This was one of the actions undertaken by the British government as an attempt to defray the high expense of the French and Indian War, waged largely to protect the interests of the colonies. However, many of the colonists objected because they had no representatives in Parliament. In the summer of that year, some of the more nonplussed did as all calm, rational firebrands do: A group calling themselves the Sons of Liberty protested the act under the elm, hanging two tax collectors in effigy. Mind you, massive riots were a common enough occurrence in Boston's political life, so a symbolic act was relatively placid in comparison. From that day on, residents called the elm the Liberty Tree, and it became a rallying point, because an illegal gathering could be explained away as a casual occurrence. Separatists in the other colonies took up the idea and formed their own Sons of Liberty, each appointing a local tree to be a meeting point. The original Liberty Tree lasted until the last day of August in 1775, when a group of Boston loyalists cut it down and used it for firewood. This was like throwing more fuel on the fire, and the Liberty Tree became a symbol on flags used by the American forces. Even though the tree is long gone, you can see where it once stood, near the intersection of Washington and Boylston Streets. You'll see a relief plaque on the third floor of the Registry of Motor Vehicles, and across the street from it is an additional bronze relief, added when people realized that an original marker was filthy, obscured, and covered in bird droppings. At least no one had to rake the leaves in the fall.

The Right Stuff-ing

Chinatown

When Boston's beloved toy emporium FAO Schwarz went belly up in 2003 after more than 125 years of delighting children, the owners and the city were faced with a bear of a problem: what to do with the 3-ton bronze bear icon in front of the Back Bay store.

Boston being Boston, there were historic considerations to debate and discuss. Should the bear be moved? If so, where? And exactly how do you transport a giant teddy that's 12 feet tall and 8 feet wide?

Suggestions poured in from some seven thousand children in thirty-four states and five countries. Finally, after a year of mulling (mauling?) it over, a new site was selected in front of the Floating Hospital for Children at Tufts–New England Medical Center. The hospital was founded in 1894 as a hospital ship sailing in Boston Harbor. In 2004 a giant crane cradled the cuddly, humongous bear and transported it to its new home.

Sculptor Robert Shure (who also created Boston's Irish Famine and Ted Williams memorials) created the bear back in 1991 when the bull market was strong and FAO was stuffed with funds. You can visit the bear at the entrance to the Floating Hospital at 755 Washington Street.

The Joke's on You
Chinatown

Did you hear the one about . . . ? You can fill in the blank any way you want, because the American Comedy Archives at Emerson College probably did. In 2004 alum Bill Dana, a well-known comedian in the 1960s who eventually became head writer on the *Steve Allen Show,* came to the school with the suggestion that it start an archive of American comedy comprising manuscripts and interviews with comedians. So far, the oral history part of the project includes interviews conducted with such comedy legends as (in alphabetical order so we aren't accused of choosing the top banana) Bea Arthur, Shelley Berman, Lewis Black, Dick Cavett, Phyllis Diller, Larry Gelbart, Charles Grodin, Buck Henry, Don Knotts, Rose Marie, Gary Owens, Tom Poston, Carl Reiner, George Schlatter, Betty White, and Jonathan Winters. All told, there are sixty-four completed interviews, with transcripts and videos on hand. These aren't recitations of jokes, but personal anecdotes and backstage insights into how comedy works. (Where else can you see what Louis Nye had to say about working with Jack Benny, Bob Hope, and Steve Allen, or Don Knotts talking about working for the first time with Andy Griffith on Broadway in the show *No Time for Sergeants*?) But the collection faces a problem. Emerson funded the undertaking at first, but now it needs to raise money to continue the noble effort. Just remember, if you decide to participate, no funny money. The Comedy Archives are part of the Emerson College Library Archives at 120 Boylston Street. Drop-ins aren't allowed, but you can get the current contact to make an appointment, or learn more about the archives and read some interview excerpts, by going to www.emerson.edu/comedy/about/History-of-the-Archives.cfm.

★ ★

Founding Father and Sun

Chinatown

The Boston Lodge of the Chinese Freemasons is located at 6 Tyler Street. Founded in 1868, the lodge played a pivotal role in a historic revolution. Like the Freemasons just around the block a century earlier who led the American Revolution (see "Freemasons No Longer Stonewalling"), Boston's Chinese Freemasons set the stage for the overthrow of the corrupt Qing dynasty, which had ruled China for 250 years.

In 1905 Dr. Sun Yat-sen traveled to the United States to raise money for his fellow revolutionaries in China. Arriving in Boston in 1910, he hid and slept in the basement of the Freemasons' lodge. In a secret rendevous in the basement of 12 Tyler, he met with seven men, five laundry workers and two restaurateurs. It was from this underground headquarters that the men plotted strategy and raised the money that flowed from the Chinese-American community to the revolutionaries in China.

In 1911 Sun Yat-sen returned to lead the revolt establishing the Chinese Republic on the "double ten"—the tenth day of the tenth month.

Portraits of the founding fathers George Washington and Dr. Sun Yat-sen hang side by side in the auditorium of the Chinese Consolidated Benevolent Association of New England, at 90 Tyler Street.

Congressional Downfall

Chinatown

Wilbur Mills was the chair of the U.S. House of Representatives Ways and Means Committee from 1957 to 1975, served in office from 1939 to 1977, and had the reputation of being the most powerful man in Congress. The Arkansas Democrat even ran for president in 1972. One of the driving forces behind Medicare, he outlasted opponents and the political weather for decades, until a dalliance brought him down. In October 1974, the U.S. Park Police stopped him in

Washington, D.C., for involvement in a traffic accident and driving at night with his lights off. Mills was allegedly drunk and had a cut on his face from a fight with Annabelle Battistella, a stripper from Argentina better known as Fanne Foxe. In the car with him were Foxe and three other passengers. Mills leaped out of the car and tried to escape, but officers took him into custody, and he ended up at St. Elizabeth's Mental Hospital. Still, the next month he was reelected to office with 60 percent of the vote. However, at the end of November, he found himself brought onstage by the "Argentine Firecracker" in the Pilgrim Theatre, smack in the middle of Boston's red-light district, nicknamed the Combat Zone. The sixty-five-year-old talked to the audience for a bit; then Foxe pecked him on the cheek, and he was off the stage and out of a political career. He told reporters that he had gone up to Boston to prove that he wasn't cheating on his wife of forty years and having an affair with Foxe. Talk about your miscalculation! House members were upset, and Mills had to step down from his committee chairmanship, out of real power faster than an exotic dancer's tassel could spin. He acknowledged a problem with alcoholism, got treatment, and started devoting his time to helping other alcoholics. He did not seek reelection in 1976. Taking his seat in Congress was Jim Guy Tucker, who would go on to become governor of Arkansas and then resign in disgrace when convicted of fraud in the Whitewater scandal. The Pilgrim, which eventually turned into an X-rated movie house, was demolished in 1996. You can see the site of the house that took down a member of the House at 658 Washington Street.

Fully Baked

Dorchester

Those who have done any amount of home baking are probably aware of Baker's Chocolate, one of the standard names in kitchen confections. But long before General Foods (which later merged with Kraft) bought the company, it was a venerable greater Boston institution. John Hannon was an Irish immigrant in the mid-eighteenth century with a kinship for cocoa. Although without a penny to his name, he knew how to process cocoa beans into chocolate, and he also could run a chocolate mill. A number of attempts had been made in New England, but none survived in the long run, even though residents were as chocolate mad then as they are today and the process of manual grinding was considered difficult even in those days of hand whisking and chopping. In 1764 Hannon had a chance meeting with Dr. John Baker. Hannon had the know-how and Baker, the money to invest. The two went into business, purchasing an old sawmill on the Neponset River in Dorchester. Business was brisk, and they opened a second mill, each operating one of them. But they fell out and became competitors. Years later, in 1779, Hannon would disappear for good, whether shipwrecked on a trip to buy beans or skipping out on his wife, no one would know for sure. Baker's business grew, as did his facilities. General Foods would buy the company in 1927 and finally close down the plant in 1965, moving operations to Delaware. But the mill still exists, now converted into condominiums. You can see it, and a historical marker, at 1231 Adams Street.

Passing Grass
Dorchester

Boston would seem to have had a love affair with Richardsonian Romanesque architecture, given the number of buildings that feature it. One that might seem a stretch, though, is the Calf Pasture Pumping Station. Pumping as in sewage. In the 1880s, open cesspools, and the diseases they brought, were still a common sight in parts of Boston, so the city implemented what would be a wonder in waste management. It installed sewers throughout and, in 1883, connected them all to a central point—the pumping station in Calf Pasture, named for the area's history as grazing land. Powerful pumps would move the sewage through a tunnel that ran out to Moon Island, finally dumping the material into storage tanks. As the tide went out, so went the sewage, unfortunately added to the bay. The plant kept working for over eighty years, until it was finally replaced by a new treatment plant on Deer Island in Boston Harbor in 1968. The station looks something like a castle, which makes sense, as it was connected to so many porcelain thrones. You can take a rest stop at 435 Mount Vernon Street and see it yourself.

Sorry, Wrong Number
Downtown

Around Boston you'll find numerous plaques and monuments heralding Alexander Graham Bell's invention of the telephone, for which the U.S. Patent Office issued Bell patent number 174,465 on March 7, 1876. The patent is considered the richest in the history of invention. There's just one small problem: Bell didn't invent the telephone. Historians now say he probably stole it.

At the time, Scottish-born Alexander Bell was living in Boston and teaching at Boston University, toiling in his downtown lab with devices that could help the deaf to hear and communicate. Bell couldn't get his device to work. In fact, it wasn't until three days after he received his patent that the box transmitted the now famous words, "Mr. Watson, come here . . . I want to see you." Bell was successful only after visiting the Washington patent office and seeing the patent application of another inventor, Elisha Grey, which depicted a liquid transmitter. The two inventors applied for their patents on the same day, but Bell received the government's approval.

Bell was courting the deaf daughter of one of the most powerful attorneys of the day, Gardiner Hubbard, who lived in nearby Cambridge. It seems a lawyer in Hubbard's Washington office was a friend of the patent examiner. The examiner, in a sworn statement, said he received $100 from Bell and showed him Elisha Grey's drawings. Lawsuits went nowhere, and Bell always denied the payment.

Bell loved to demonstrate his "invention," and on May 4, 1877, he placed the first long-distance phone call between Boston Music Hall

One of many markers wrongly attributing the first telephone to Alexander Graham Bell.

and his loyal assistant, Thomas Watson, who was in Somerville 5 miles away. Tablets marketing the approximate location of the invention of the telephone are at 7 Avenue de Lafayette, off Washington Street.

Dental Plaque
Downtown

At the corner of Tremont Street and Hamilton Place, you'll find a plaque honoring Dr. W. H. Stowe's contribution to the world of dentistry. Dr. Stowe had a thriving private practice in Boston but was even better at making false teeth. Like a grin, his reputation spread far and wide, and in 1887 the good doctor, later joined by his cousin Frank Eddy, opened the nation's first commercial dental laboratory.

The dental plaque is mounted on the wall at the corner of the

A toothsome smile in front of Boston's Dental Plaque.

FedEx building diagonally across from Brimstone Corner, where colonists once hid gunpowder in the crypt of the Congregational church that is located there. The church is also where the hymn "America" was first sung (July 4, 1831); the country's oldest musical organization, the Handel and Haydn Society, was founded; and William Lloyd Garrison began his long career as an abolitionist.

The Hub of the Universe
Downtown

Bostonians are a self-centered lot, and why not? After all, the city's immodest nickname is The Hub, as in "the hub of the universe." The phrase is actually derived from something Oliver Wendell Holmes wrote in *The Autocrat of the Breakfast-Table* about the capitol building: "Boston State-house is the hub of the solar system. You couldn't pry that out of a Boston man if you had the tire of all creation straightened out for a crow-bar."

★ ★

You may have to move a box of fruit to find the Hub of the Universe.

Since Holmes wrote this whimsical collection of essays in 1858, the so-called center of the universe has moved a bit. You'll now find it near Filene's Basement on a spot marked with a bronze plaque about 15 feet from the store's Washington Street entrance. Perhaps fitting for its top banana status, in order to see the center of the universe, you might have to move a bunch of bananas or two . . . and perhaps some onions and a crate of oranges. The plaque, marking the hub of the universe, is now in the center of a fruit market at 426 Washington Street.

★ ★

Ben Franklin: Founding Farter

Downtown

The statue of Benjamin Franklin on School Street is one block from Milk Street, where Franklin was born in 1706. It was the first portrait statue erected in Boston and marks the site were Franklin attended the first public school in the United States.

The four sides of the statue feature images of Franklin the patriot, the printer, the inventor, and the diplomat. If you look closely, you might detect a sly smile on Franklin's face. Old Ben, well known for his keen, irreverent wit, once wrote a satirical piece flaunting the benefits of flatulence. In his essay "Fart Proudly," Franklin, the founding farter, proposed eating a food additive "that shall render the natural Discharges of Wind from our Bodies, not only inoffensive, but agreeable as Perfumes."

A sly Ben Franklin has a mischievous air about him.

45

★ ★

Perhaps the base of Franklin's statue should have had five sides. But we shudder to think what it would have looked like.

Revolutionary Rolls
Downtown

Hotels make for strange bedfellows. John Wilkes Booth, Malcolm X, Ho Chi Minh, Ralph Waldo Emerson, and John F. Kennedy all spent time at Boston's Parker House.

Now known as the Omni Parker House, it is the oldest continuously operating hotel in the continental United States. When it opened for business in 1855, it was the first hotel in Boston to have hot and cold running water and an elevator. John Wilkes Booth stayed here the week before he shot Abraham Lincoln. Ralph Waldo Emerson, Nathaniel Hawthorne, and Henry Wadsworth Longfellow were members of the famous literary Saturday Club, which regularly met in the hotel's restaurant. Had the wordsmiths assembled some eight decades later, Malcolm X might have cleared their table; he worked as a busboy in the hotel restaurant in 1940.

The Parker House is famous for its rolls. Legend has it that this gastronomic delight is the happy result of an angry chef. The Parker House prided itself on meeting the needs of the pickiest patron, but in 1856, when one particularly demanding guest made one too many requests for a certain roll, it is said that a hotheaded German chef began throwing small balls of dough into an oven. Surprisingly, the rolls were delicious, and the talk of delighted guests gave rise to the famed Parker House roll. The hotel kept the recipe a secret until President Franklin Roosevelt requested it in 1933.

The Boston cream pie (which is actually a cake) was also concocted here. The origin of the pie/cake is not entirely certain. Some say it was created by a French chef named Sanzian. There is no truth to the story that the misnamed dessert was part of a Communist plot to confuse American diners, although revolutionary Ho Chi Minh did work as a baker at the Parker House from 1911 to 1913.

⭐ ⭐

The Parker House is also where John F. Kennedy proposed to Jackie Bouvier (table 40), announced his candidacy for the U.S. Congress in 1946, and gave his first speech. At the age of six, while attending a celebration for his grandfather, John "Honey Fitz" Fitzgerald, the former mayor of Boston, the young president-to-be told the crowd, "This is the best grandfather a child ever had."

For a taste of Old World charm, and to imagine what it must have been like way back when chefs were tossing dough and bakers were plotting coups, check out or check into the hotel at 60 School Street; (617) 227-8600; www.omnihotels.com/FindAHotel/BostonParkerHouse.

The Man Who Invented Money

Downtown

Long before Wall Street financier Bernard Madoff made $60 billion and headlines with his pyramid scheme, there was Charles Ponzi, whose name is synonymous with the get-rich-quick con.

Ponzi was a small man with a taste for the finer things in life. He loved luxurious houses and large automobiles, and he dressed in the finest suits, with top hat and walking stick. Too bad he couldn't afford them. No matter; the former dishwasher, convicted smuggler, and scam artist was "the man who invented money." At the peak of his pyramid scheme in 1919, Ponzi was raking in $1 million a week. He created 40,000 "millionaires" and at one point sauntered into the Hanover Trust Company, opened a suitcase with $3 million in cash, and bought a controlling interest in the bank.

The pyramid scam is probably as old as, well, the pyramids. But it took Charles Ponzi, an Italian immigrant living in Boston, to raise it to new heights in the world of modern finance. The scam is simple: Borrow from Peter to pay back money you borrowed from Paul. Repeat over and over again and, voila, you have a Ponzi scheme. A bit like Social Security, the system works as long as you bring in enough new

investors at the bottom to support those at the top of the pyramid.

Ponzi employed a new twist on the old scam. He promised investors a 50 percent return on their money in ninety days if they purchased international postal reply coupons, which were coupons he bought overseas for a penny and exchanged in the United States for six cents. (Unfortunately, it wound up costing more money to ship and exchange the coupons than they were worth here, but that was a minor detail to Ponzi.)

Ponzi's house of reply coupons finally collapsed when a Boston newspaper questioned the con. Ultimately, five banks went belly-up in the scam. Ponzi wound up spending seven years in a Boston jail and died penniless in Rio de Janeiro. He left behind an unfinished manuscript for a book, appropriately titled *The Fall of Mr. Ponzi*.

Ponzi's office was on the fifth floor at 27 School Street.

Party Animals
Downtown

In front of Boston's Old City Hall are two unique monuments to the city's rich and contentious political heritage. The bronze donkey statue stands opposite footprints with elephant figures embedded in the sidewalk, symbolizing an ongoing relationship.

Over the years thirty-eight mayors served their terms on this site. Perhaps the most colorful, James Michael Curley, served part of his term as mayor in federal prison. Although Democrats have never accepted the donkey as their party's symbol, all twenty of Boston's Democratic mayors did. The GOP officially adopted the elephant as its symbol, but only five of the ten Republican mayors went with the party pachyderm.

The plaque next to the donkey and footprints tells the story:

In 1828 Andrew Jackson established the Democratic Party and ran for president using the populist slogan "Let the people rule." His opponents thought him silly and labeled him a "jackass." Jackson, however, turned their name calling to his advantage by using the donkey on his campaign posters. Over the years, the donkey has become the de facto symbol of the Democratic Party.

The symbol of the Republican Party in 1874 was born in the imagination of a cartoonist, Thomas Nast, in *Harper's Weekly*. Soon other cartoonists used the elephant to symbolize Republicans, and, eventually, Republicans adopted the elephant as their official symbol.

While you're pondering whether to ride the jackass or stand in opposition, you may want to hop out to the front sidewalk and try out the hopscotch board mosaic. It recognizes this as the site of the first public school in America, Boston Latin School, established in 1635.

You can catch the menagerie at 45 School Street.

Political parties take fixed positions in front of Boston's
Old City Hall.

★ ★

Pregnant Building

Downtown

Where do little shacks come from? Why, from pregnant buildings. At least, you might think that when you see the First National Bank Building, otherwise known as the Pregnant Building. At 591 feet, it's Boston's sixth-tallest building, but clearly height isn't the only distinguishing characteristic of a structure. The architecture is of the so-called Brutalist style that started in the 1950s and lasted until the 1970s: lots of angles, lots of concrete. It has been called an abomination, though, as we mention elsewhere in this book (see "World's Ugliest Building"), the current City Hall, also in the Brutalist style, is far uglier. But it is a building that sticks out, both literally and figuratively, creating a sense that it is either pushing all neighboring structures out of the way or trying to avoid being bumped into. Even from blocks away, looking down Congress Street from near Faneuil Hall, it stands out. The reasoning behind the bulge made sense. The architectural firm Campbell, Aldrich & Nulty wanted to expand space on the street for pedestrians. Fair enough. Unfortunately, when you walk past the Pregnant Building, you can't help but feel that there's something looming over you … because there is. If you want to see the Pregnant Building, head toward 100 Federal Street. We guarantee you can't miss it. Unless it has gone into labor and is off in the delivery room.

Yvonne's Eats

Downtown

Boston's emergence as a multifaceted culinary destination worthy of a stop is recent. In the eighteenth century, dining meant a pub or private residence. But by the early twentieth century, fine food and drink would mean French and Locke-Ober. In the 1870s, Luis Ober ran Ober's Restaurant Parisien on Winter Place with funds forwarded by Eben Jordan, cofounder of the Jordan Marsh Company, once a major retailing force in the area. Over time he would vastly renovate the space, adding hand-carved mahogany furnishings and bar, French glass mirrors, a decorated ceiling, and etched gold wallpaper. Perhaps the most famous appointment, though, is a painting of a woman who came to be known as Mademoiselle Yvonne, who is always *au naturel* except when a Harvard team loses to Yale, in which case the painting is draped with black crepe.

In 1886 a different type of competition reared its head in the form of Frank Locke, who set up a neighboring cafe called Frank Locke's Wine Rooms. Both proprietors left the area in 1894—Ober retiring on a fortune he had amassed, and Locke dying at age forty-six that year. Business partners bought both establishments and knocked down the wall between them, calling it the Winter Place Tavern. Eventually, Emil Camus, who worked at the establishment for a couple of years before heading to California, returned to form the Locke-Ober Company, secured the services of the chef who worked for years with Ober, and created a local institution. The restaurant has undergone some renovations and changes of ownership over the decades. It wasn't until the 1970s that women were allowed to dine at the restaurant, even though Yvonne still tended bar, so to speak. Ironically, Chef Lydia Shire, a fixture of Boston cuisine and onetime sous chef to Jasper White, now runs the kitchen with Chef Mario Capone. You can try the food, and see the artistic patroness, at 3 Winter Place. For information call (617) 542-1340 or visit www.locke-ober.com.

Doing the District Shuffle

Downtown

Chicago may brag of its political machines and machinations, but remember that Boston has been at the game since before the country was founded. Sam Adams was one of the original rabble-rousers, literally stoking mobs into laying waste to buildings and scaring the living daylights out of those in power. But in 1812 the commonwealth gave birth to a new concept born of democracy: gerrymandering. Elbridge Gerry was the governor of Massachusetts from 1810 to

★ ★

1812. A signer of the Declaration of Independence and the Articles of Confederation—and notably one of three men who refused to sign the Constitution without a Bill of Rights—Gerry apparently had no problem using laws to ensure political advantage. In 1800 he joined the Democratic-Republican Party. In 1812 he realized that he could lend a hand to his chosen party and so indulged in redrawing some legislative districts, creating something described as having the shape of a salamander that would provide advantage to a Democratic-Republican candidate. The *Boston Gazette* ran an editorial cartoon and coined the term *gerrymandering* as a description of the practice. Gerry's party is long gone, but his name lives on in political infamy. There is a plaque at 176 Arch Street commemorating the invention.

Aging Skyscraper

Downtown

Say *skyscraper,* and you think of buildings whose stories run up into the dozens. In the nineteenth century, though, construction was less ambitious. The Ames Building was Boston's first skyscraper, and it is still standing. When it was completed in 1893, it was a towering thirteen stories tall. Although it was a first in the city, it never got to be the officially tallest building. In those days, church steeples were counted as part of a building's height, and taking that into account, the Church of the Covenant in Back Bay towered over the Ames. Making the building taller would have been tough, as these were the days before construction used internal steel frameworks, limiting how far up you could build. But it has other claims to fame. The Ames Building is the second-tallest building in the world supported solely by masonry walls, which are 9 feet thick in the Ames. (The tallest one was built the same year in Chicago.) It was commissioned by Frederick L. Ames, whose company made shovels used in building Civil War fortifications and the transcontinental railroad. The Richardsonian Romanesque building (see "All Washed Down") was designed by Shepley, Rutan & Coolidge. The base of the building is granite, sandstone, and brick. Some years back, the building was unoccupied. But you can't just tear down an edifice that is on the National Register of Historic Places. Luckily, it has been renovated to become a hotel with an upscale restaurant. For a good look at a building that has aged gracefully, go to 1 Court Street.

John Hancock's Hand

Downtown

You'd think a guy who was president of the Continental Congress, who signed the Declaration of Independence, who almost single-handedly financed much of the American Revolution out of his own pocket, who provided barrels of wine for the crowds during political

You gotta hand it to Hancock—he had a great signature.

Build with the Force

(Cue the John Williams music.) One Exeter Place stands out in contrast to its neighbors. It towers over all the nearby red brick and brown sandstone buildings and is largely black, with an aggressive mansard roof. Built in 1984, it acquired the nickname "the Darth Vader Building."

demonstrations in Boston in the 1760s, and who was the governor of the Commonwealth of Massachusetts over multiple terms might get some respect. And John Hancock did when he was alive, as he inherited his uncle's mercantile fortune and was the second wealthiest man in the American colonies in his financial prime. But, oh, how soon they forget. Like the minute you're in the ground. Hancock died in his fifty-sixth year in 1793. His good friend Sam Adams, who was acting governor at the time, declared a state holiday, and he was sent off with a lavish funeral and then interred in the Old Granary Burying Ground. Then the gloves came off. Or at least the hand, according to the popular legend. The night he was buried, grave robbers supposedly snuck in and severed the hand he used to sign the Declaration. No one would have been keeping watch over the Burying Ground, as it wasn't until the 1830s or so that people thought of graveyards as places of remembrance, and not just a place other than the parlor to park a corpse. You can find a sign near his grave in the Old Granary Burying Ground on Tremont Street, just a block or so away from King's Chapel.

You Need This Museum like a Hole in the Head
Roxbury

The Warren Anatomical Museum is the kind of place to which Alfred Hitchcock might have brought a first date. The museum is fascinating in a macabre sort of way and not without humor, with a vast collection of medical instruments, photos, anatomical models, machines, gadgets, specimens, body parts, and medical memorabilia. In all, more than 13,000 artifacts detail the evolution of modern medical science from the nineteenth century. The collection of gallbladder stones, preserved conjoined twin fetuses, and Peruvian skulls are among the museum's highlights. You'll be astonished by how far medicine has come in such a short period of time . . . and perhaps be unnerved by just how primitive it was until not too long ago.

★ ★

Dr. John Collins Warren started collecting unusual anatomical specimens in 1799, when he was just twenty-one years old. In 1848 he
hung up his stethoscope (there are scores of models on display) and
resigned his Harvard professorship, donating his world-class collection
of weird artifacts to the medical school. His own skeleton is now part
of the collection.

On display is the phrenological collection of Dr. Johann Gaspar
Spurzheim, who studied skull bumps for clues about personality and
brain function. In 1832 the famed German doctor died unexpectedly
in Boston while on a lecture tour. His body is buried in Mount Auburn
Cemetery in Cambridge, but his unusually large skull is on display at
the Warren Museum.

The most popular exhibit is the skull of Phineas Gage. An on-the-
job accident sent a 13-pound steel bar flying through Gage's cheek
into his brain. Unexpectedly, Gage survived. His memory was intact,
but his personality took a turn for the worse. He became mean and
lost his social constraints. Scientists studied Gage's skull for clues
about personality. Seems they needed just such an accident, like a
hole in the head, to discover the inner workings of the brain. The
Warren Anatomical Museum Exhibition Gallery is on the fifth floor of
the Countway Library of Medicine, 10 Shattuck Street. For information call (617) 432-6196 or visit www.countway.harvard.edu.

Spurzheim's tomb is at the intersection of Fountain and Lawn Avenues, left side, adjacent to the road in Mount Auburn Cemetery, Mount
Auburn Street, Cambridge. Watch out for the bumps in the road.

Statue Ping-Pong
South Boston

Artists beware: When people in Boston don't like your work, they're
likely to do something about it—even if your creation is a 3,500-pound,
27-by-18-foot aluminum sculpture. Polish émigré Andrzej Pitynski created the work called *The Partisans,* a group of five weary and hag-
gard riders that commemorated Poles who fought both the Nazis

✦ ✦

and Communists and, through them, all freedom fighters. Pitynski loaned the statue to Boston in 1983. It was supposed to be placed at City Hall Plaza, but then-outgoing mayor Kevin White was reportedly concerned that that could have been interpreted as his leaving office in defeat. Instead, he had it placed on the Boston Common, facing Charles Street, where it was unveiled on November 10 of that year, as White declared it Partisans' Day. That may have mollified feelings over its being relegated to a secondary spot, but over the next twenty-three years, arts officials were miffed that they hadn't given official approval for the location; local residents thought it was depressing and not in the theme of American history that much of the art on the Common takes up. Some even said that it was a danger, as people would climb on the statue during public events. So in January 2006, the city carted off the sculpture and put it into storage. Then came the protests from the Polish-American community. Later that year, the MBTA, which runs mass transit in the region, said that it had a site in South Boston, and eventually the statue was placed on a little-traveled stretch of road that arcs between the new Boston Convention and Exhibition Center and the old World Trade Center. And, hey, if they need to move the statue again, the subway is always handy. To see what is actually a fine piece of sculpture, park by the Convention Center on Summer Street at World Trade Center Avenue. Walk up the latter and look to your right to see *The Partisans,* hopefully to retreat no longer.

Got Milk?

South Boston

The Hood Milk Bottle, on the plaza in front of the Children's Museum at 300 Congress Street, is no pint-sized display. The wooden bottle was built in Taunton, Massachusetts, in 1933 and shipped to Boston in 1977. It's 40 feet high, 18 feet in diameter, and could hold 58,620 gallons of milk, making for one very big milk mustache. During the summer it also serves as an ice-cream stand and snack bar. Check out www.bostonchildrensmuseum.org.

Gallons of fun can be found at the Children's Museum.

Tanks Vermilion, Ho Ho Ho Chi Minh

South Boston

The world's largest copyrighted work of art is on permanent display just south of downtown Boston in Dorchester on I-93. It's the so-called Rainbow Tank, a 140-foot-tall liquid natural gas tank featuring five huge stripes of color: vermilion, orange, yellow, blue, and purple.

In 1971 Boston Gas commissioned artist Corita Kent to paint the tank. Kent, a former nun best known for designing the famous Love postage stamp, said the Rainbow Tank was an expression of peace. The war in Vietnam was raging, and Kent was a peace activist.

Ho Ho Ho Chi Minh has the last laugh.

★ ★

Some say they can see evidence of Kent's antiwar sympathies hidden in the tank. Look at the middle stripe. See the profile of Ho Chi Minh? Who? Ho Chi Minh, the former leader of North Vietnam and a busboy at Boston's Parker House Hotel (see "Revolutionary Rolls") in the 1920s. Others say the roadside Rorschach test contains the image of the devil, Osama bin Laden, or Fred Flintstone. And then there are those who say that sometimes a tank is just a tank. It can be seen about 2 miles south of Boston on I-93. Be careful: Don't use the access road leading to the tank. It's private property. There are remote cameras watching you, and the property owners will call the police if you are on the road.

Gillette Employees Get Worked Up into a Lather

South Boston

Back in 1901 traveling salesman King Camp Gillette developed the world's first double-edged disposable blade, and the hirsute have never been the same. Today, from its World Shaving Headquarters in South Boston, where Gillette founded his international empire, the company turns out blades by the billions. To ensure that the company lives up to its claim that Gillette's razors are "the best a man can get" and that they get even better, Gillette employs some five hundred engineers and scientists in laboratories around the world who send their improvements back to Boston for evaluation. The shaving lab is a top-secret place. No cell phones or cameras are allowed.

More than three hundred volunteers at the South Boston factory sign up for the shave-in-plant program to test-drive the latest experimental models. Each morning men from a select group take off their shirts, enter one of twenty booths, and lather up. Technicians in white lab coats register their reactions as the men shave the right side of their faces with one unmarked razor and the left side with another. The results are entered into a computer. After decades of studying shaving and blades under electron microscopes and in slow motion, Gillette has come to understand that making a blade shave smoother

✦ ✦

than a baby's bottom takes a lot more than science and technology. Because it sells blades from Armenia to Zanzibar, Gillette has to be sensitive to different kinds of skin and hair types, as well as to cultural differences. Over the years, shaving scientists have learned that what constitutes a great shave is really a subjective experience; there's the sound of the blade slicing through whiskers, the feel of the razor in the hand. After all the testing and experimenting, it turns out that when it comes to shaving, beauty is in the eye of the beard holder. The World Shaving Headquarters is at 1 Gillette Park in Boston.

Now, Where Did I Put That Key?

South Boston

The giant Fortress padlock is a familiar, neck-bending icon for motorists on I-93. When fully inflated, the 700-pound lock is 32 feet tall and 20 feet wide. To make sure the blow-up lock doesn't blow away, it's taken

The giant padlock seen on I-93 just south of Boston.

down for the winter and stored—where else?—in the super-secure, climate-controlled Fortress storage facility.

The eight-story Fortress building at 99 Boston Street is also unique. Fortress, the largest provider of high-security storage in the United States, invented a giant carousel device that suspends the room-sized safety deposit vaults in midair and automatically delivers them to clients waiting in the lobby. The giant lock is in good company. Many museums use Fortress to store their works of art.

Revered Artist
South Boston

Anyone who has gone to grade school in the United States has at one point or another likely seen the famous engraving that Paul Revere did of the Boston Massacre. However, he had some unwitting and ultimately angry help. Henry Pelham, the half brother of famous Boston portraitist John Singleton Copley, was an artist in his own right. After the Boston Massacre, he drew his re-creation of the scene. But in those days, copyright was an unheard of concept, and Revere was a man who knew his way around metalwork and making a buck. He made a poor engraving of Pelham's drawing, and by three weeks after the event he was advertising copies for sale. Moving far more quickly than Pelham, he scooped up the money to be had before the artist could get his own work out on the streets. Not only did he steal the design, but he made some significant changes to it, having a colorist paint a blue sky even though the event took place at night and Revere had left a crescent moon in view. He also decided to eliminate the figure of Crispus Atticus (or Attucks), an African American killed in the fray, replacing him with a dog. A few incendiary touches ensured the popularity of the image, and there was the prominent addition at the bottom that the picture was sold by Revere. As you might imagine, Pelham was angry about the whole affair and accused Revere of robbing him "as truly as if you had plundered me on the highway." You can see the actual copper engraving plate that Revere himself cut on display at the Commonwealth Museum. Although small, the museum has some other interesting exhibits, including the original charter for the commonwealth and other rare historic documents.

The state's archives have an equally interesting, if more prosaic, collection of items. Some of the odder ones were turned up by archaeologists working alongside excavators on Boston's Big Dig (the largest public works project in history), including the oldest bowling ball in North America. If that doesn't bowl you over, perhaps this will: They found the ball under the floorboards in a "house of office," the seventeenth-century term for a privy. The oak ball is flattened on two sides and is about the size of a grapefruit. It has a perforated middle to hold a lead weight to give the ball more play when rolled. Not that play was what the Puritans had in mind when they founded Boston: A statute was passed in 1646 forbidding bowling because it caused "much waste of wine and beer." Perhaps a bowler taking a nip too much might explain why the ball was found in the toilet. While not exactly a gold mine, Katherine Nanny Taylor's privy is an archaeologist's treasure trove. The seventeenth-century toilet also contained 250,000 seeds and fruit pits along with 158 fragments of silk, ribbon, and lace.

The Commonwealth Museum and Massachusetts Archives are at 220 William T. Morrissey Boulevard. Follow the signs for UMass and the JFK Library. The State Archives Building, which houses the Commonwealth Museum, is across from the JFK.

We Can't Hear You
South End

Musicians will tell you that Boston's Symphony Hall is one of the finest in the world because of its superior acoustics. And when it was built, the design was revolutionary. The Boston Symphony Orchestra had been playing since 1881 at the old Boston Music Hall, which was known, among other things, for a massive pipe organ. But that

building was threatened by road construction in the late nineteenth century, so the city built a new home for the orchestra, Symphony Hall.

The architectural firm entrusted with the design was McKim, Mead & White. Up until then, the design of musical spaces was art, not science. But there had been extensive work done in the new study of acoustics, much of it started by the physicist Wallace Clement Sabine, an assistant professor at Harvard. He had never set out to become the leading expert in sound, and didn't even have his PhD, but he found himself asked to improve the sound in the Fogg Lecture Hall, part of the Fogg Art Museum, when more senior members of the faculty declined the task. Over several years, Sabine and assistants carried out meticulous tests both at the Fogg and at the acoustically lively Sanders Theatre. He eventually found that by intelligently deploying absorbing materials, he could control the reverberation time and balance a room between echo and flat sound. (The unit of sound absorption, the sabin, is named for him.)

The architects hired Sabine to be the acoustical designer. During the project, he had the opportunity to travel to Leipzig and investigate the Neues Gewandhaus, a music hall with an international reputation for excellent acoustics. Between his work in reverberation and his chance to see how the Gewandhaus was constructed, Sabine brought his intellectual gains to work with McKim, Mead & White to choose a closed box hall rather than an open-air theater and to use specific materials and construction techniques.

The result is a hall still considered one of the best venues in the world for classical music. For all his knowledge of acoustics, Sabine was no businessman. He never did get paid for the Symphony Hall work. And even though he earned more than half of his 1909 Harvard salary in consulting fees, he was notoriously bad at business matters. He insisted that a building's owner pay his $200 consulting fee and would return checks sent by the involved architectural firms. According to an article in *Millimeter* magazine, one client said, "I was very much impressed with the complete absence of any commercial instinct in Professor Sabine's makeup."

Ironically, the Boston Music Hall (not to be confused with the Music Hall, which would eventually be called the Wang Theatre) was never torn down, and it eventually became the Orpheum Theatre. The organ was also saved and now sits in Methuen Memorial Hall in Methuen, Massachusetts. You can take in the results of Sabine's expertise at Symphony Hall, 301 Massachusetts Avenue, or visit www.bso.org.

Play Ball
South End

Fenway Park is synonymous with the Red Sox and baseball in Boston. But it only opened in 1912, and baseball is older. The game was first professionally played in the city in 1871 by the Boston Red Stockings, which, ironically, would *not* become the Red Sox. The team was good, winning four of the first five championships of the National Association of Professional Base Ball Players. One of its pitchers, Al Spalding, would go on to found the sporting goods company.

In 1883 the team changed its name to the Boston Beaneaters to avoid confusion with the Cincinnati Red Stockings. To get a sense of what things were like, in their first season in 1894 they played 132 games, winning 83, before a total attendance of 152,800. Eventually, the team would change its name several more times with some changes of ownership: first to the Doves, then the Pilgrims, and finally, in 1912, to the Boston Braves. The club won the 1914 World Series, had some disappointing seasons, but did see some brushes with greatness. They added legendary athlete Jim Thorpe to the roster in 1919 and hired a forty-year-old Babe Ruth in 1935.

The next year, the team name changed again, to the Bees, and Casey Stengel eventually took over as manager. More mixed results and another name change followed, this time back to the Braves, with lots more disappointment. The team was actually in Boston

until 1953, at which point it was relocated to Milwaukee. One of the places they played was the South End Grounds. For a view of where it was, go to the William E. Carter playground on Columbus Avenue, between Camden and Burke Streets, and look southeast to where fields once rang with the sweet crack of a bat hitting a ball. For more on the history of the Braves, go to www.sportsecyclopedia.com/nl/bosbraves/BosBraves.

The First World Series
South End

It was 1903. Baseball's National and American Leagues had been slugging it out for the market, and it only left them both bruised. So they decided to stop fighting and create some kind of final game of the season in which the champion of each league would meet to determine who was best for the year. Facing each other for a nine-game series were the Boston Americans and the Pittsburgh Pirates. The Boston team, which had Cy Young on its pitching roster, would end up getting its fifth win during game 8, which was played in the Americans' stadium, the Huntington Avenue Baseball Grounds. And so, the team that would become the Boston Red Sox won the first World Series. Games on the Huntington Grounds would see twenty Hall of Fame players, including Ty Cobb and Connie Mack. Cy Young threw the first perfect game in the modern baseball era there. Although the stadium is long gone, you can see where sports history was made. Go down St. Botolph Street toward Gainsborough and keep going until you run out of road to find yourself in the middle of what once was the Huntington Avenue Baseball Grounds.

3

Brahmin Boston

Prepare yourself for *a transfusion; you're about to enter blueblood territory. Some of the windows on Beacon Hill are even, well, not blue, but purple. Now there's a neighborhood that encompasses the span of Boston's experience, from what author Henry James called "the only respectable street in America," much of which was on land essentially bilked from the famous portraitist John Singleton Copley, to the birthplace of free African-American communities in the country. There's the birth of American football in America's oldest public park and what used to be the world's shortest suspension bridge. There's religious persecution perpetrated by the Puritans, right after they escaped such bigotry in Europe, as well as the home of the woman who wrote "The Battle Hymn of the Republic." Thank goodness someone gave military endeavors a good name, because in front of the Massachusetts State House—which is the home of the Sacred Cod and Holy Mackerel—is a statue of the general who lent his name to practitioners of the world's oldest profession.*

★ ★

Rights Etched in Stone

Beacon Hill

America almost didn't get off the drawing boards as a country. Ratification of the U.S. Constitution fell into serious trouble in Massachusetts. John Adams, John Hancock, and Elbridge Gerry (see "Doing the District Shuffle") refused to sign the document until it contained language protecting individual freedoms. By then five other states had already ratified the document with ease, but other states were waiting to see what Massachusetts did. Under what became known as the Massachusetts Compromise, delegates recommended to the new congress language that would include a Bill of Rights if states ratified the Constitution.

Today, the first ten amendments are etched in stone in the Bill of Rights Walkway in Pemberton Square near the Old Courthouse in downtown Boston. The sidewalk sculpture features a mosaic of ten Roman numerals, one for each of the amendments in the Bill of Rights. Each numeral is outlined in brass and is embedded with small letters expressing the text of the corresponding amendment to the Constitution. The walkway was installed by the Boston Bar Association to commemorate the bicentennial of the Constitution of the United States in 1990. You can find it at 16 Beacon Street.

For Whom the Bell Tolls

Beacon Hill

King's Chapel is situated on the public burying ground because no Boston resident would sell land for a non-Puritan church. Originally an Anglican church, it was built in 1688 and made of wood. In 1749 the current stone structure, using rock from the nearby Quincy quarry, was built. The stone church was constructed around the wooden one. When completed, the wood church was disassembled and the parts removed through a window. The wood was sent to Nova Scotia to construct another Anglican church.

During the American Revolution, King's Chapel was called the Stone Chapel by disgruntled colonists.

The church had a bell from the very beginning, but it cracked. A second bell, weighing 1 ton, was made in London in 1772 and rang until May 8, 1814, when a sexton cracked that one while ringing it. Paul Revere and Sons melted the bell and recast one weighing 237 pounds without the clapper. This was the last of 400 bells cast by Revere. According to legend, the bill of sale bears a notation by the famous silversmith/midnight rider: "This is the largest and sweetest bell we ever made."

The bell is still rung for two services on Sunday and noon service on Wednesday. King's Chapel is at 58 Tremont Street; (617) 523-1749; www.kings-chapel.org.

The sweetest-sounding bell can be found in Boston's King's Chapel.

Riders of the Purple Pane
Beacon Hill

With its reputation for being a straight-laced town, Boston has always shown glimpses of its wild side, and some of the more interesting, if lesser noticed, examples are the windows in some of the older houses. If eyes are windows to the soul, then what are windows themselves? Some are downright purple. For example, look at the Appleton-Parker House, a historic building at 39–40 Beacon Street. It, like some other buildings, was constructed with windows that had too high a concentration of manganese oxide in the glass. Over

In the Poor House

There are few addresses more prestigious, or more expensive, than the stately houses lining the Beacon Hill portion of Beacon Street. But at one point, this was not a desirable location for the gentry. Beacon was once known as Poor House Lane because the Boston Alms House stood on it, on the corner where Beacon and Park Streets intersect. What set off the attraction of the area was a land deal that came at the expense of John Singleton Copley. The famous portrait artist once owned much of the land in the area. But he permanently moved to London in 1774 to pursue the further study of art and eventually brought his family over. Of course, it didn't hurt that all of his family seemed to consist of Loyalists. His agent in Boston allowed himself to be persuaded to sell off Copley's extensive real estate holdings on Beacon Hill for $1,000 an acre. This was a steal, and Copley was unable to stop the transaction before it took place. The real estate speculators who spent a total of $18,000 built mansions and generally cleaned up.

time, what was originally expected to be clear glass turned a shade of purple, clearly the slow but steady development of the structure's wild child. Of course, in the case of the Appleton-Parker, you might expect as much, given that the land was once owned by painter John Singleton Copley and owner Nathan Appleton married off daughter Frances to poet Henry Wadsworth Longfellow in the house. (Numbers 34, 63, and 64 on Beacon also have passionate panes.) A more idiosyncratic approach can be seen at 24 Pinckney Street, designed by the nephew of Ralph Waldo Emerson, in which no two windows are the same size.

The Man Who Married Himself
Beacon Hill

We can only imagine how Puritan tongues did wag when members of the humorless sect learned that their own governor, Richard Bellingham, married himself.

In 1641 (1651 according to some sources), when Bellingham was about fifty years old and recently elected governor of the colony, the widower remarried. His bride, Penelope Pelham, was just twenty-two years old and the second granddaughter of Lord De La Warr, for whom the state of Delaware is named. Pelham was reportedly quite a looker, and Bellingham first got sight of her when she was being wooed by a young man living in the governor's home. By now the tongues were going full speed. Not only was the Gov stealing another man's object of desire, but instead of announcing his intention to wed publicly, as required by colonial law, Bellingham performed the ceremony himself. In other words, he married himself. Bellingham was also a magistrate, so he could tie the marriage knot. Puritans challenged the legality and brought charges against the governor, but the indictment was soon dropped. Seems, as a judge, Bellingham could also preside over his own trial.

Bellingham served as governor three times, and the couple lived happily ever after. The same cannot be said for Bellingham's sister,

Can You Top This

You would expect a statehouse to be crowned by a symbol of the state, but in the case of Massachusetts, you'd be wrong. Atop the magnificent gold dome of the Massachusetts State House in posh Beacon Hill is a gilded pinecone. The white pinecone and tassel is the state flower of Maine. When this section of the statehouse was completed in 1798, Maine was a district of the Commonwealth of Massachusetts. Maine didn't gain its independence from Massachusetts until 1820, as part of the Missouri Compromise. So Maine may be gone, but the pinecone remains. Top that.

Maine's state symbol is on top of the Massachusetts State House dome.

Anne Hibbins. Boston Puritans executed her as a witch in 1656.

Bellingham Place is just off 85 Revere Street. There are only four houses on the dead-end cobblestoned street. Bellingham Place is just the most recent name for it. Prior to 1885, it was known as Sherman Place, then May Street Court and Hill Street. Governor Bellingham never lived anywhere near the street that now bears his name.

Oldest African-American House
Beacon Hill

Old buildings are nothing new in Boston, and one of the more notable ones is the Middleton-Glapion House at 5–7 Pinckney Street. Its lesser claim to fame is as the oldest standing private home on Beacon Hill. More importantly, it is the oldest existing house built by African Americans. It was originally constructed by George Middleton, who was a coachman but had been a Revolutionary War colonel, and Louis Glapion, a barber or hairdresser who may have been from the French West Indies. The friends bought the property for 30 pounds in 1786 and had built the two-family house by 1791. Although the now private residence was originally a 345-square-foot, one-story structure with two windows, a second story was eventually added. Two off-center doors and the larger window on the left of the first floor match the original recorded description of the house.

A Thin Tome from the Tomb
Beacon Hill

James Allen's autobiography is one book you can definitely judge by its cover. It is awful, inside and out. Allen admits he was a rotten scoundrel, and the book cover testifies to that. His autobiography is certainly him: The book is bound in his skin.

In 1833 Allen attempted to rob John Fenno Jr. near Powderhorn Hill in Chelsea. Fenno fought back and was shot, but he survived because the bullet hit the buckle on his suspenders. Allen was

James Allen's autobiography is a gruesome
book from cover to cover.

arrested and sent to prison, where he wrote an autobiography of his troubled youth and his life as a highwayman.

Allen died on July 17, 1837, but before he did, he asked to meet with Fenno, saying he wanted to shake the hand of a brave man. Then he made his fateful request. Figuring that once he was dead it would be no skin off his nose—or actually his back—Allen asked that a copy of his autobiography, bound in his skin, be given to Fenno and a second copy be given to Dr. Bigelow of Boston, the physician he requested attend his death.

Allen's skin was removed, and bookbinder Peter Low tanned his hide and edged it in gold. The binding looks like pale gray deerskin and is inscribed in Latin *Hic Liber Waltonis Cute Compactus Est* ("This book by Walton bound in his own skin"). The full title of the book is *Narrative of the Life of James Allen, Alias George Walton, Alias Jonas Pierce, Alias James H. York, Alias Burley Grove, the Highwayman. Being His Death-Bed Confession, to the Warden of the Massachusetts State Prison.*

Allen's autobiography was donated to the Boston Athenaeum by one of John Fenno's descendants, and you can still find it there today, but the copy given to the doctor has never been found. The Boston Athenaeum (617-227-0270) is located at an address Harry Potter would love: 10½ Beacon Street. The Athenaeum's collection includes 600,000 volumes. James Allen's autobiography is the one most often requested. You can access the text of the thin tome on the Athenaeum's Web site at www.bostonathenaeum.org.

The Only Respectable Street
Beacon Hill

There are bad addresses; there are good addresses. But according to Henry James, if you're in the United States, you want to be on Mount Vernon Street in Beacon Hill. The writer called it "the only respectable street in America," and who are we to argue? For a street on Beacon Hill, it is wide, with lovely homes and a stately presence that is

palpably different from any other part of the area. Whatever the coin-
cidences responsible, there is a uniformity to the houses on the street,
with keen architectural detail, attractive design, and a visual rhythm
that adds a pleasing unity to the neighborhood. Away from the
stretch on which James lived, just a few blocks from Charles Street,
Mount Vernon borders Louisburg Square, one of the most desired
locations in the city. Go to 131 Mount Vernon, right behind the State
House, and you can stand in front of the house where James and his
brother, William, lived in the mid-nineteenth century. They had plenty
of literary company. Louisa May Alcott, who wrote *Little Women,*
lived at 10 Louisburg Square, just a few doors from a former *Atlantic
Monthly* editor, William Dean Howells. Julia Ward Howe, who wrote
the words to "The Battle Hymn of the Republic," lived at one point
at 32 Mount Vernon, and Robert Frost, when he wasn't stopping by
woods on a snowy evening, was a onetime resident of 88. But expect
a walk that can be steep in places, with iron railings set into buildings to keep people from slipping when the brick sidewalks ice over in
winter.

The Sacred Cod and Holy Mackerel
Beacon Hill

Suspended over the entrance to the Massachusetts House of Representatives chamber is something you won't find hanging over any
other deliberative body in the world: a codfish. And it's not just any
codfish. It's the Sacred Cod. Measuring 4 feet, 11 inches, the pine
carved fish is a constant reminder of the importance of the fishing
industry to the state's early history. The Pilgrims and Indians feasted
on cod along with turkey that first Thanksgiving, and it was the
state's first export. We even named a cape after the cod.

The fish that currently holds the place of honor above the legislative body's entry is actually a third-generation cod. The first was
destroyed in a fire in 1747; the second, during the Revolutionary War.
The current one has been hanging around since 1787, moved from

Fishing may have floundered in Massachusetts, but the tradition still holds in the State House.

the old statehouse to the new House chamber in 1895. It has hung there ever since, with one notable exception. In 1933 pranksters from the *Harvard Lampoon* "codnapped" the state's seafood symbol by cutting the line holding it aloft. They made off with their prize catch hidden in a flower box. Lawmakers were outraged. The state police were called in to investigate. The Charles River was dredged. Days later, an anonymous tip led to the revered fish's recovery, and it was hung 6 inches higher to prevent it from being stolen again.

Those who say something very fishy is going on in the Massachusetts State House have a basis for their claim. In 1974 the cod was elevated to the status of official state fish. Not to be outdone by the lower house, the Senate has in its chamber a wrought-iron chandelier with a fish in its design. It's called the Holy Mackerel.

Over in the House chamber, check out the second painting on the left behind the speaker's chair. It shows one of the judges from the Salem witch trials repenting for sentencing accused witches to death. The gesture is a bit late but still appreciated; after all, it's the thought that counts. The Massachusetts State House is on Beacon Hill overlooking Boston Common on Beacon Street. Self-taught architect Charles Bulfinch designed the building, which was constructed between 1795 and 1797 on a pasture owned by John Hancock. Although it may look high now, the hill is 50 feet lower than its original height, as land from the hills was used to fill in Boston's Back Bay. The gilded dome, first made of wood shingles, is topped by a lantern and a pinecone (see "Can You Top This?"). The fish are indoors.

Fighting Joe Hooker

Beacon Hill

A statue of Major General Joseph "Fighting Joe" Hooker, on his mighty steed, stands in front of the entrance to the Massachusetts State House. One shudders to think what the statue could have looked like, considering what Hooker is best known for: lending his last name to the oldest profession. Joe Hooker was a favorite son of

Massachusetts. He commanded the Army of the Potomac during the Civil War, but Fighting Joe's men were a rowdy bunch, and Hooker's headquarters was a den of iniquity. The encampment was said to be a combination barroom and brothel. Hooker allowed women who followed his troops to set up their tents nearby. Hence, the derogatory term "Hooker's Division" became the popular equivalent for prostitutes.

There is some evidence that the word *hooker* was used before the Civil War, but the story of Fighting Joe clearly was responsible for its common use today. His statue is right in front of the public entrance to the State House on Beacon Hill, which the British referred to as Mount Whoredom.

Joe Hooker rides high but took the low road in battle.

★ ★

A First Lady

Beacon Hill

While on Mount Vernon, that "respectable street," you can see what was once the home of Julia Ward Howe: feminist, abolitionist, suffragist, and author of "The Battle Hymn of the Republic." Howe's lineage was pure blueblood, being descended from the founder and two governors of Rhode Island on her father's side and from Revolutionary War figure Francis Marion, known as the Swamp Fox, on her mother's. Her mother died when Howe was five; perhaps that helped her establish the fiercely independent spirit that would eventually make her name.

From an early age she was accomplished, learning Italian, French, German, and Greek as a child and sneaking in such authors as Balzac and Sand without her father's knowledge. Through her brother, she met Henry Wadsworth Longfellow, Charles Dickens, Charles Sumner, and Margaret Fuller. When she married, it was to Dr. Samuel Gridley Howe, who was known as the "Lafayette of the Greek Revolution" and who was founder of the Perkins Institute for the Blind. The relationship would be stormy, as Gridley expected her to stay at home and not write or work publicly. Eventually the two would separate. Howe achieved fame in her own right as a poet, author, intellectual, and political activist—and she managed it all while having seven children (and a lot of family money before her husband frittered much of it away on bad investments). The day her husband died, she wrote in her diary, "Start my new life today." She was a leader in the abolitionist, women's suffrage, and world peace movements. In her spare time, she wrote travel books, children's fiction, and music. And created Mother's Day. She also had a reputation for having a high opinion of herself. No wonder. The house is now a private residence. For more information on Howe, check out www.juliawardhowe.org.

Odd Volumes
Beacon Hill

Most book clubs are discussion groups that come together in some-one's living room. The Club of Odd Volumes is considerably more formal, and exclusive. The reason for the group's existence is to "pro-mote literary and artistic tastes, the exhibition of books, and social relations" among the members. Founded in 1887 by eighteen Boston blueblood book lovers, it was originally a dinner club in the tradition of private men's clubs, but with a twist, or maybe it should be a new leaf. The word *odd* was not added in the sense of peculiar, but refer-ring to an unmatched set.

By 1900 the Odd Volumes added members and began to run exhi-bitions and even publish its own titles. The subject matter, and the materials made available, could be quite exclusive. According to the 1904 bylaws, for example, there could only be no more than fifty-one members, with any new member requiring a unanimous vote. One exhibit catalog from the 1920s goes into detail about specific rare volumes dating from 1450 to 1600—in other words, from the begin-ning of modern book printing using movable type. Examples of such titles are generally the sort you'd have to travel to a museum or major library archive to see. There are reputedly still fewer than one hundred members in the organization, many of whom come from academia, publishing, and printing. The club is shelved at 77 Mount Vernon Street.

Dyer Straights
Beacon Hill

One of the great myths of American history is that the Puritans came to the New World to establish religious freedom. Actually, they were interested in religious freedom for everyone to believe the way the Puritans did. (Members actually left the Church of England because they considered it "impure.") One of the more shameful examples

★ ★

was how, early on, the founders of Massachusetts banned Quakers from stepping foot into their territory and were willing to hang those who did. What set off the animosity was, as so often happens, a difference in theological interpretation. The Quakers held to what became known as the Antinomian heresy, or the belief that people are saved only by faith, not good works.

If they had stopped there, that would have fit with the Puritan concept of the elect, that a divine power "saved" a chosen few and wrote off the rest of humanity, no matter how individuals behaved. But the Puritans still believed in the necessity of "good works," mostly to prove that they were part of the elect. Antinomianism, on the other hand, was based on a conclusion that if the difference between those saved and those not was predetermined, then it didn't matter what people did; therefore, they had no duty to follow codes of ethics or morality. That crossed the line with the Puritans, who banished from the commonwealth the Quakers for their beliefs.

Anne Hutchinson was high on their list of undesirables, as was one of her followers, Mary Dyer. Governor John Winthrop would eventually refer to Dyer as "a very proper and fair woman" but "very censorious and troublesome." Accompanying her husband on a trip to London, she converted to Quakerism and, on her return in 1657, found herself tossed into jail. The government eventually released her to go with her husband to Rhode Island and never to return. She did with two companions, who were subsequently hanged. After being forced to watch the two executed, things went so far as to have the hangman place the noose around her neck. But a last-minute plea from her son got her released and, again, sent to Rhode Island. Again, she returned, this time to be executed on Boston Common in 1660, making her the only woman to be executed in what would become the United States for her religious beliefs. Today there is a statue of her on Beacon Street by Park Street outside the State House. Included in the inscription is a quote: "My life [does] not availeth me in comparison to the liberty of the truth."

Free Community at Last

Beacon Hill

Boston was a birthing place for revolutions political, scientific, and religious. But it has also been the start of social revolutions as well, including the first all-free African-American community in the United States. Originally starting in the North End, families moved into the West End and the northern part of Beacon Hill. By the first census of the new U.S. government in 1790, Massachusetts was the only state to record having no slaves.

Although there are numerous sites on the Black Heritage Trail, one of the must stops is at the African Meeting House, the oldest black church building in the country still standing. Within these walls took place such historic events as the founding of the New England Anti-Slavery Society, an antislavery speech by Frederick Douglass after he was forced out of the Tremont Temple, and the recruitment of the famous all-black Civil War fighting force the Massachusetts Fifty-fourth Regiment.

Next to the meeting house is the Abiel Smith School, which was the first building constructed to be a public grammar school for black children. In 1787 the Massachusetts legislature denied a petition to allow African Americans access to public schools, so the residents organized their own classes in a home on West Cedar Street and Revere Street. The school moved to the first floor of the African Meeting House in 1808. It took another twelve years for Boston to create two schools for black children. A bequest to Boston for the education of black youth resulted in the construction and dedication of the Abiel Smith School in 1834 and 1835. The school closed twenty years later when Massachusetts outlawed segregation in public schools. You can see both the African Meeting House and the Abiel Smith School at 46 Joy Street. For more information, call the Museum of African American History at (617) 725-0022, or go to www.afroammuseum.org.

★ ★

The Parkman Bandstand
Boston Common

The bandstand in Boston Common was a gift to the city from one of its greatest benefactors whose father was the victim of one of Boston's most notorious crimes.

George Francis Parkman Jr. died in 1908, leaving $5 million to the city to care for the Common and other parks.

In 1849 Parkman's father, Dr. George Parkman, a wealthy surgeon, was bludgeoned to death and dismembered by Harvard professor John Webster. Webster had fallen on hard times and borrowed money from Parkman. When Parkman tried to collect, Webster murdered the Boston Brahmin and placed his body parts behind a brick wall. His body was discovered, and his wife identified the body by markings on his penis.

Webster's crime and trial were international sensations. Sixty thousand tickets were sold to the trial in which Webster was found guilty and hanged. George Francis Parkman went into seclusion in the family mansion at 33 Beacon Street. A plaque honoring the philanthropist can be found there. Exactly 150 years to the day that Dr. Parkman was murdered, a cistern on the third floor of the home flooded the newly renovated house. The Parkman Bandstand is in Boston Common near Tremont Street.

Charlie and the MTA
Boston Common

Boston's subway was the first in the nation. It opened in 1897, and riders have been getting lost ever since. Officially it's the MBTA (Massachusetts Bay Transit Authority), although locals simply call it the T. But in 1959, it gained momentary fame when the folk singing group The Kingston Trio recorded a hit song called "Charlie on the MTA," about "the man who never returned" from a ride on Boston's subway because he didn't have the money to pay the exit fare (at the time, some stops required payment to leave the train). So every day his wife would wait and hand him a bag of food. Why she didn't include the extra nickel we'll never know.

The song was actually written a decade earlier, running nine pages long, as a campaign tune when Walter A. O'Brien ran for mayor on a platform to simplify subway fares. O'Brien had the song played from a sound truck. He lost the race and was fined $10 for disturbing the peace. O'Brien left Massachusetts and moved to Maine, becoming the politician who never returned.

For those with a bit more than a nickel, the T lines are color coded. The Red Line used to end at Harvard University, whose official color is crimson. The Orange line is named for Orange Street, which was

Mosaic mural by Lilli Ann Rosenberg on the outbound Green Line at Park Street Station.

under the once-elevated stretch and is now known as Washington Street. The oldest section, the Green Line, runs adjacent to the string of parks known as the Emerald Necklace, and the Blue Line runs under Boston Harbor.

All Mine

Boston Common

Today, land mines are rightly considered a scourge of society and one of the most unpleasant gifts that wars keep on giving. But mines, at least at sea, did not always suffer such a dark reputation. During World War I, a total of 56,571 mines were laid in what was called the North Sea Mine Barrage in an attempt to halt the effectiveness of German submarines.

Although an early submarine was used in the American Civil War, this was the first time that countries saw what an advanced form of the vessels could do, sinking traditional warships with a single torpedo. The original plan of the Mine Barrage was to lay 70,177 mines throughout the 250-mile North Sea Strait that ran between Norway and Scotland. A total of thirteen U.S. ships were involved over a five-month period. The work was horribly dangerous, given that the ships, packed with mines that were a yard across and containing 300 pounds of TNT, had to work in the rough North Sea waters. Captain Reginald Belknap, who was in charge of the actual mine-laying operations, said that "mines were constantly at one's elbow," and eventually wrote his wife that "interesting as these trips are, no sane person would take two for pleasure." Five percent of the mines went off when they were set or shortly after.

Although the original number of mines was not set, by the time the mission was done, the crews had mined a swath of ocean 230 miles long and 15 to 35 miles across. The Mine Monument was presented to the city by the North Sea Mine Force Association in 1921. You can find it on the Boston Common near the Civil War Memorial. For more information about the Mine Barrage itself, point a browser to www.worldwar1.com/dbc/nsminebr.htm.

Football Takes Flight
Boston Common

Boston is a big sports town, with the Celtics, Red Sox, and Bruins. The local football team, the Patriots, is quartered a good distance away in Foxboro, but the city wasn't always bereft of regular pigskin passing. In 1862 Boston saw the first organized football team in the country, the Oneida Football Club. For three years, the club "played against all comers" without giving up a single goal. Notice that we're not going to enter the argument of whether the game they played was American football as we know it now or a variation of soccer, which is called football in the rest of the civilized world. The reason is that there is no way anyone could know: The playing rules of neither game was set at the time, so there's little chance that what the Oneida Club played resembled anything we would recognize today. Chances are that what it played was a hybrid called at the time the Boston game. In one way it doesn't matter, because the Oneida Club was apparently the first group outside England to use the term *football.* Also notice that organized was not the same as professional, as the players were largely secondary students from the city's public schools, like Boston Latin. They had to do something while waiting for pro sports drafts. There is a small monument, placed in 1925 by seven surviving members, to the Oneida Club on the very fields on which it played, near the intersection of Walnut and Beacon Streets.

Wherefore Art Thou, Romeo?
Public Garden

See those two lovebirds floating in Boston's Public Garden lagoon? A happier pair of swans you'll not find. When they were introduced, Bostonians had high hopes the couple would swoon and make the first ever cygnets. The city began keeping swans in 1989 but had no luck hatching babies.

One spring, the lovebirds began standing guard around nine eggs. Hearts lifted, voices rejoiced, but, alas, no little birdies emerged. One by one the eggs disappeared. Finally, park officials had the remaining egg inspected. It hadn't been fertilized. It seems instead of Romeo and Juliet the city had gotten Juliet and Juliet. Swans of the same sex can lay eggs, but it takes a male to fertilize them.

A year after the swan discovery, Massachusetts became the first state in the nation to allow same-sex marriage. Swans mate for life, so Juliet and Juliet will live here in Boston, happily ever after. It brings to mind the nineteenth- and early-twentieth-century term for two women living together without a man supporting them: a Boston marriage.

Historic swan boats ply the straight and narrow in Boston Public Garden.

Ether or Either

Public Garden

Boston printer Gilbert Allen never knew what hit him. After a few whiffs from an ether-soaked sponge, he was out. When he woke up, the human guinea pig learned he had made medical history. It was October 16, 1846, and Gilbert Allen was the first person to be successfully operated on while under anesthesia. Before then, undergoing an operation had meant enduring excruciating pain. Now, the ether-assisted surgery proceeded in silence as an astonished crowd of physicians looked on. Afterward, Dr. John Warren, the surgeon who performed the operation, told his incredulous colleagues, "Gentlemen, this is no humbug."

Bah, humbug, indeed. The operation touched off a controversy of competing claims over who actually had invented the potent stuff, with two Boston dentists taking credit. When city authorities proposed a monument memorializing the inventor, they consulted Harvard physician and wordsmith Oliver Wendell Holmes. It was Holmes who coined the term *anesthesia* and, acting Solomonlike, suggested dedicating the statue to "either or ether."

When Mark Twain learned that neither man would be named on the statue, he proclaimed that the ether monument "is made of hardy material, but the lie it tells will outlast it a million years." Well, either it will or it won't, but it has lasted since its unveiling in 1868 in the Boston Public Garden. It is the oldest monument in the country's oldest public park. The Ether Memorial can be found facing Arlington Street. Atop the red marble columns is a rendition of the Good Samaritan. Be sure to check out the weird reliefs behind the granite arches.

The surgical amphitheater in which the first anesthesia-assisted operation took place is called the Ether Dome. It was designed by the great architect Charles Bulfinch. Until 1873 it was used as an operating room. Then it served as a storage area, a dormitory, and a dining room for nurses. It is now a classroom. The Ether Dome is open to the public and is located at Massachusetts General Hospital, 55 Fruit Street.

Patients breathed a lot easier after the invention
of ether. This monument in the Boston Public
Garden pays homage to the painkilling gas.

Stars, Stripes, and Bars

In 1941, to commemorate the tenth anniversary of "The Star-Spangled Banner" as the U.S. national anthem, Russian émigré Igor Stravinsky reorchestrated the song. Unfortunately for the composer, the song, originally penned by Francis Scott Key, was reharmonized off-key and violated a Massachusetts law forbidding any "tampering" with the national ditty. Stravinsky's performance reportedly left the audience "stunned into bewildered silence." Boston's finest visited Stravinsky at a later concert to make sure there wasn't a repeat performance. One Boston newspaper quoted Captain Thomas Harvey as saying, "Let him change it just once, and we'll grab him." The law is still on the books in Massachusetts.

In 1918 German-born Karl Muck, conductor of the Boston Symphony Orchestra, also got stung by the "Banner." Muck was nabbed by federal agents for refusing to lead the orchestra in the tune. He said it wasn't in accord with the serious compositions in the schedule. The BSO stripped Muck of his position, and he was interned during World War I as an enemy alien.

Keeping Bridges in Suspense
Public Garden

As far as we're concerned, it's all water under the bridge, but just to set the record straight, the Boston guidebooks have it wrong. Despite what they say, the iron bridge that crosses the swan lagoon in Boston Public Garden is not the world's smallest suspension bridge. When it was built in 1866, the span, a quaint fifty-six paces long, was indeed a suspension bridge, but repairs in the early 1900s turned it into a plain old bridge.

★ ★

The world's smallest suspension bridge isn't.

Boston's newest bridge, the Leonard P. Zakim Bunker Hill Bridge, emerging from the underground Central Artery near Causeway Street, may also look like a suspension job, but it's not. It's a cable-stayed bridge. In fact, it's the widest cable-stayed bridge in the world. Both a suspension bridge and a cable-stayed bridge use two towers, but there is a difference in how the cables are attached to the towers. In a cable-stayed bridge, the cables run directly between the roadbed and the towers, and the towers bear the load. Suspension bridges have the cables slung over the towers, and they transfer the load to the anchorages on the other side.

While you are trying to figure out the difference, check out the new bridge's towers. They look just like the Bunker Hill Monument to the east. The bridge is named after the famous battle and for Lenny

Zakim, a Jewish activist who tried to bridge the difference of Boston's many racial, religious, and ethnic communities. For his work, Zakim was even named Knight of St. Gregory by Pope John Paul II in 1999.

What's Up, Duck?
Public Garden

Robert McCloskey's *Make Way for Ducklings* is Massachusetts's official children's book. The children's classic features Mr. and Mrs. Mallard's darling little ducklings: Jack, Kack, Lack, Mack, Nack, Ouack, Pack, and Quack. A 38-foot-long bronze sculpture of the jaywalking ducklings and their mom can be found in the northeast corner of Boston Public Garden. The statue, sculpted by Nancy Schön,

Make Way for Ducklings is all it's quacked up to be.

was installed in 1987 and quickly became a favorite of residents and visitors alike. Then in 1999 someone "ducknapped" Jack. Bostonians, usually unflappable about such matters, were incensed. Thankfully, a month later the statue was found under a desk at a Boston college. But the ducknapper had sawed Jack's legs off just above his webbed feet, so a new Jack had to be made. The one in Boston Public Garden is the new Jack. The old Jack, with his legs repaired, now has a new home at the rooftop playground outside Boston Medical Center's pediatric department at 84 Harrison Avenue.

4

Back Bay

If sometimes you *feel as though you're under water when trying to understand some of the odd things in Boston's Back Bay, don't feel too bad. This is an area built largely on landfill. One church actually had to be rebuilt to keep from tipping over, while another needs to have water poured on its foundational pilings to keep them from rotting away. There's a mansion festooned with mythological creatures, a diorama of the history of the environs, one building known for a famous falling grape, and another infamous for falling windows. The Back Bay includes the birthplace of Edgar Allan Poe and a dormitory allegedly haunted by the spirit of Eugene O'Neill. Maybe he's tormented by the idea of being able to order a $12,750 martini. You can even stop by a museum to see a couple of pictures that no longer hang there.*

The Lotta Dumb Animal Fund Fountain
Back Bay

A lot of thirsty dogs, cats, and horses owe Lotta Crabtree a debt of gratitude. Crabtree funded the canine fountain you'll find on Boston's Charles River Esplanade.

The 6-foot-high dog oasis was built in 1939. The sculpture was done by Katherine Weems, who modeled the dog atop the fountain after her own pet. The dog looks down on a cat spout. Weems also carved two larger-than-life rhinos on the front steps of Harvard University's biological lab.

Charlotte "Lotta" Mignon Crabtree was a childhood actress from New York who traveled around the country with her mother and two huskies. Seems the young actress was a cross between Mae West and Shirley Temple. The *New York Times* described her as "the face of a beautiful doll and the ways of a playful kitten."

Lotta's mom would purchase properties in cities where the Belle of Broadway performed. When her mother died, Lotta moved to Boston. She never married and lived alone in a hotel with her dog at her feet and a cigar in her mouth. She amassed a fortune, and by the time she died in 1924, she was the second-largest taxpayer in the city. Once the vice president of the Massachusetts Society for the Prevention of Cruelty to Animals (SPCA), she left $300,000 to establish the Lotta Dumb Animal Fund, which paid for the fountain.

The fountain has fallen into disrepair. The face on the cat spout is half removed. In 2004 a state probate judge removed the fund's trustees, ruling they had paid themselves hundreds of thousands of dollars from Crabtree's estate but spent just $100 to maintain the fountain. Obviously, it's a dog-eat-dog world. The Lotta Fountain can be found halfway between Berkeley and Clarendon Streets just off Storrow Drive, not far from the statue of Einstein's head.

★ ★

The Plywood Palace

Back Bay

Building the sixty-story John Hancock Tower, Boston's tallest sky-scraper, was a real "pane in the glass." In 1973, soon after workers began installing the first of 10,344 windows, the panes began to crack, and many of the windows fell to the ground. Luckily, no one was killed or injured. The entire exterior of the 790-foot building had been designed to be covered in special mirror-glass, but by April 1973, plywood had replaced more than an acre of the tower's high-tech windows. The building became known as the Plywood Palace.

Needless to say, lawyers had a field day—or, in this case, field years. There were lawsuits and countersuits and counter-countersuits. Scientists and engineers were perplexed. After much high-tech

The Hancock Building was dubbed the Plywood Palace after workers replaced fallen windows with sheets of wood.
Photo courtesy of Peter Vanderwarker

✦ ✦

sleuthing, the problem was identified. However, the judge in the case imposed a gag order on the aggrieved parties that lasted seventeen years. It was not until 1990 that the public learned what was wrong. It seems that the bonding material that was supposed to hold the dual layers of insulated glass together didn't.

All 10,344 windows were replaced with single sheets of tempered glass. Sensors were installed on each pane to provide an early warning if any pane began vibrating too much. Five thousand undamaged windows were sold to the public for $100 each. As for the plywood, it was used to board up abandoned buildings in the city. The Hancock Tower is located on Clarendon Street and St. James Place near Copley Square. You can't miss it. It's the one with all the shiny windows.

Leaning Tower of Boston
Back Bay

Soon after the New Old South Church was completed in 1873, the massive 260-foot-tall tower, or campanile, began to tilt. By the 1920s the tower was 3 feet out of plumb and threatening to topple onto Boylston Street. In 1931 the leaning tower of Boston was dismantled stone by stone and rebuilt slightly shorter to its present-day 240 feet.

The church is a world-class example of Northern Italian Gothic architecture, but it's a Yankee Doodle original. The exterior facade is made of Roxbury puddingstone, and the structure was designed by two local architects, Charles Amos Cummings of Boston and Willard T. Sears of New Bedford.

The exterior is decorated in a stripe-and-checkerboard style and features carvings of squirrels, owls, and birds among the vines. Architects Cummings and Sears were so proud of their design, they immortalized themselves in stone. Look at the archway to the right of the main door on Boylston Street. Above you'll see the biblical message "Behold I have set before thee an open door." Carved into the pillars holding up the porch under the words *have* and *thee* you'll find the faces of Cummings and Sears. The one on the left has a beard.

The New Old South Church in Boston isn't new, and it isn't in the South. The original congregation met at the Old South Meeting House in downtown Boston, which was in what was then Boston's South. The meetinghouse is famous as the site where rebellious "Indians" launched the Boston Tea Party. The address is 645 Boylston Street. Call (617) 536-1970 or visit www.oldsouth.org.

The New, New Old South Church tower.

Let It Snow, but Please Don't Flash Red
Back Bay

Many cities have lights above a building that flash different colors to forecast the weather. Boston's is different. It also warns when real trouble is brewing: when a Red Sox game has been canceled. Above the Art Deco Old John Hancock Tower built in 1947 is a pyramid-shaped roof topped with the forecasting beacon. The light shines a different color depending on the weather. Clear blue means a clear view, flashing blue means clouds due, steady red means rain ahead, and flashing red means snow . . . or today's Red Sox game has been called off. If seeing from afar isn't enough, the building is on 200 Clarendon Street.

The Hancock Beacon signals whether the weather is good or bad at Fenway Park.

Finally Finished Line
Back Bay

No, that's not some weird middle-of-the-street, multicolored cross-walk on Boylston Street between Dartmouth and Exeter Streets. That's the finish line of the world's oldest annual marathon. The 26.2-mile Boston classic is held on Marathon Monday, the third Monday in April.

The Boston Marathon is so competitive that even the race has won awards. *Guinness World Records* says a record 38,708 official entrants completed the centennial running of the race in 1996. In 1980 runner Rosie Ruiz was the official finisher who never started the race. She was the first woman to cross the finish line but was later disqualified when it was learned she took the subway and jumped into the race a half mile from the end. Victory for her was certainly no sweat.

Whew! It's a race to the finish line in the marathon of marathons.

The first woman to actually run the Boston Marathon was Roberta Gibb in 1966. Gibb won the race in 1966, 1967, and 1968 but wasn't recognized for her victories. Women were not recognized as official entrants until 1971. Gibb hid in the bushes at the start of the race, jumping onto the street at the starter's gun. In 1967 runner Katherine Switzer applied as K. Switzer on the entry form and received an official bib. Four miles into the marathon race, codirector Jock Semple saw Switzer, ran into the road, and tried to pounce on her, screaming, "Get the hell out of my race, and give me that race number." Switzer's boyfriend threw a body block on Semple, who sailed through the air, and Switzer went flying down the street, finishing the race in an unofficial four hours, twenty minutes.

Medieval Mansion
Back Bay

In Back Bay, there are stately homes, impressive homes, historic homes. But we know of only one that transcends time itself because the building clearly belongs in the Middle Ages. Albert Cameron Burrage was a lawyer and industrialist of the late 1800s and early 1900s who eventually got caught up in an antitrust action of the Teddy Roosevelt era. When not working on charitable causes and civic issues, he was an avid horticulturist, being a president of the Massachusetts Horticulture Society and the first president of the American Orchid Society. But as refined as his tastes in flowers might be, what he liked in architecture could be considered . . . unusual.

The Burrage Mansion, designed by famous architect Charles Brigham and built in 1899, was based on the Vanderbilt House in New York. But you might be forgiven for seeing it as not so much a building as a roost for the unusual. The exterior, as counted by the *Boston Globe*, is festooned with forty-seven dragons, sixteen gargoyles, thirty cherubs, three figures reading books, six human heads, four lion's heads, two eagles, and assorted griffins, dragon heads, and chimeras, to say nothing of human faces and cherubs on the

What Goes Around Comes Around

Michael Killian can ride circles around other bicyclists, both coming and going. The Irish-born artist invented the sideways bicycle when he was living in Boston in 1999. His first test rides in Boston's Arnold Arboretum were memorable failures. He fell over backwards on the prototype, nearly killing himself, and still has the scar on his leg to show for it.

But Killian went straight back to the drawing board and came up with another design for the sideways bike, which, he says, "was like picking up a glove and finding it fit perfectly." He made three prototypes, painted them bright orange, and headed straight, er, sideways down the road. His comings and goings around town earned him stares and provoked reactions from astonished onlookers. Some called his contraption a Dr. Seuss mobile and Killian "the Einstein of Bicycles."

Inventor Michael Killian and his two-way bicycle.
Photo courtesy of Michael Killian

A deal to manufacture the sideways bike fell through, and Killian moved back home to Ireland, where he still tools around with his reversible ride.

Clearly, in Boston, what goes around comes around. The sideways bike is only the latest in a long, distinguished history of bicycle firsts in the United States. In 1819 an early two-wheeler dubbed the "velocipede" was built by Ambrose Salisbury in the city. It was a commercial failure. However, things really took off on May 24, 1878, when Boston was the scene of the nation's first bike race and bike club. You could say the hub of the universe has many a spoke.

wrought-iron gates. These days it is an assisted living community. You can gaze at the wonders at 314–316 Commonwealth Avenue, at the corner of Hereford Street.

Running Walkway
Back Bay

Boston has been a running town for decades, particularly when it comes to the annual marathon, and it has long taken the greats to heart. But the interest today doesn't quite capture the fanaticism of a couple of decades past. Residents treated such runners as Bill Rodgers, Joan Benoit Samuelson, and Johnny Kelley like stars. Literally. Just as Grauman's Chinese Theatre in Hollywood had movie idols put their foot- and handprints into cement, in 1984 Boston created the Walkway of the Running Stars to honor these marathon winners and others. It was situated just outside the old Eliot Lounge, which was the unofficial watering hole for the running crowd. Less than ten years later, the city tore up the walkway and, with it, all the imprints. So much for commitment.

But marathoners are nothing if not persistent, and they tried another, if smaller, version of the walkway when the concrete was recast. Times do change, and the Eliot closed in 1996, giving way to the Eliot Hotel. You can still see some faint traces of the walkway and stand in front of the old location of the Eliot Lounge by going to the intersection of Massachusetts and Commonwealth Avenues, where the hotel now stands. Go to the Mass. Ave. side and look down.

Weir Going Fishing
Back Bay

The whole of Back Bay was once so much swamp, and one of the best reminders was a series of archaeological discoveries in what would become one of the tonier shopping areas of Boston: fish weirs beneath Boylston Street. These structures, used thousands of years ago, were sets of vertical poles that held netting made of plant material. The Boylston Street Fish Weirs first came to attention when crews were digging in 1903 to build the first of the city's subway lines. Workers found sharpened stakes that were obviously not building pilings. It wasn't until the 1930s that archaeologist Frederick Johnson and a team began more systematic excavation at the old New England Life Building, obtaining a body of data about the finds and bringing them to the attention of other academics.

The discoveries of additional fish weirs continued into the 1990s. All in all, at least 65,000 fish weir stakes, dating from 4700 to 3700 B.C., have been found scattered over a two-acre area of what was marsh and mudflats. Some outlying stakes have been estimated to be older than 5,000 years. That structure suggests how the weirs were used. High tide would bring water, and fish, into the marsh. As the tide ebbed, fish would find themselves trapped in the weirs, ready for more efficient and convenient retrieval than tossing nets or shooting arrows, though not as easy as going to a nearby restaurant. Those with a hankering to fish, at least for atmosphere, can go to Boylston Street, between Berkeley and Clarendon Streets.

Once upon a Midnight Frogpondium

Back Bay

Although Edgar Allan Poe pondered weak and weary and died in Baltimore, the master of the macabre was born in Boston in 1809. Orphaned as a child, Poe lived in Boston only a short time, returning briefly in 1827 when he enlisted in the U.S. Army under the name Edgar A. Perry. While Poe was in Boston, his first book of poems, *Tamerlane and Other Poems,* was published, written anonymously "by a Bostonian." Poe had a love–hate relationship with Boston and may have been reluctant to have his name attached to the city of his birth; he often referred to Boston as "Frogpondium" after the frog pond on the Common. Perhaps appropriately, Poe's exact birthplace is in dispute. Some put it at 33 Hollis Street; others say it was on Carver Street, which is now called Charles Street South. To avoid the dispute, the plaque honoring Poe is near 176 Boylston Street. And now, 160 years after his death, the city where he was born has decided that it had overlooked its native son and dedicated Poe Square, the intersection of Boylston and Charles Streets, right by both the Boston Common and Public Garden.

Running of the Brides
Back Bay

Filene's Basement's notorious bridal gown event has been likened to the running of the bulls at Pamplona. But according to the store's PR person, Pat Boudrot, some years it's more like a prizefight, as brides-to-be go head to head in an attempt to grab a designer wedding gown at a bargain-basement $249. Some of the women arrive with

The running of the brides stampede in search of budget wedding dresses.

retinues that include their moms and matrons of honor, ready to do battle. Boudrot says they come wearing boxing gloves and chomping on mouth guards. It's a knock-down, no-holds- or clothes-barred fight to the finish as the gals make a mad dash for the dresses, stripping themselves and the racks bare in a flash. The record, witnessed by a CBS news camera team, is just thirty-six seconds. It's a scene that makes the floor of the New York Stock Exchange look like, well, a walk down the aisle.

Filene's Basement (426 Washington Street) first emptied its warehouse of designer gowns for the one-day sale in 1947. Since then, on at least five occasions, starry-eyed women, with their sights set on a "baaaahhhgain," have broken down the doors to the store before they were opened.

The objects of their affections are dresses that come from manufacturers' overstocks, canceled store orders, and, of course, canceled weddings. The gowns may retail for up to $10,000 and sell for as low as $199 on this one lucky day. One memorable gown featured a peacock hand-painted in pastels; another had a map of the world laid out in Mercator projection on the skirt.

Marketing professors Ellen Foxman and Susan Dobscha have made a cottage industry of writing scholarly papers about the sale. One of the papers, "Women and Wedding Gowns: Exploring a Discount Shopping Experience," is in the *Proceedings of the 1998 Conference on Gender, Marketing, and Consumer Behavior.* The bargain basement was closed for remodeling at press time but slated to reopen when the work is done. Until then the stampede is being held at nearby Hynes Convention Center, 900 Boylston Street.

The Christmas Tree Is the Present

Back Bay

If you want to see the most magnificent Christmas tree in the nation, forget about the ones at the White House and New York's Rockefeller Center. They dim in comparison to the one in Boston. For more than thirty years, Boston's official Christmas tree in Boston Common has run rings around any and all competitors. But don't take our word for it. The seasonal symbol comes from Nova Scotia, Canada, the self-proclaimed "Balsam Fir Christmas Tree Capital of the World," as an annual gift selected after a six-month search. By tradition, the tree has to be at least fifty years old and 50 feet tall.

The tree is a present from Halifax, the provincial capital, for the help Boston sent to the city during its time of greatest need. In early December 1917 a ship filled with munitions exploded in Halifax harbor. It was the largest artificially created explosion in history until the detonation of the atomic bomb. Halifax was flattened; thousands were killed and injured. Boston citizens braved a blizzard to deliver food, medical aid, and supplies to the city, and Halifax has never forgotten.

In 2005 the Hub's tree caused quite a hubbub. When the city's Web site referred to the evergreen as the "holiday" tree, the evangelist Jerry Falwell saw red. Reverend Falwell, who died in 2007, mobilized his flock. Falwell's fundamentalist faithful bombarded Boston City Hall with a half million e-mails. Boston's mayor, not wanting to appear like the Grinch who stole Christmas, quickly had the reference removed, and soon all were merry.

The traditional lighting of Boston's official Christmas tree takes place in early December in Boston Common.

Model Citizens
Back Bay

If you're interested in how the Back Bay became what it is today, then the old New England Financial Building has something for you. Inside the lobby are four detailed dioramas. These are not your children's school projects. Commissioned by the New England Life Insurance Company and created by Sarah Anne Rockwell, who learned about diorama construction as an art student, each started with months of research. She worked not only from historical texts, but

★ ★

actually went back to original blueprints, re-creating each building and element to accurate scale. The work was painstaking, as it took Rockwell two weeks to make a single human figure and a month to complete a horse. Reproducing the Museum of Natural History was a seven-month project in itself. Her level of detail was not limited to external appearances, but to activities as well. For example, there are small figures of workers transferring sand and gravel by cart from the trains where they arrived to fill in the broad spaces between tempo-rary tracks and created graded surfaces for construction. One of the dioramas even includes a reconstruction of the fishing weirs described elsewhere in this chapter (see "Weir Going Fishing"). For a chance to tower over the development of Back Bay, go to the lobby of 501 Boylston Street.

What a Grape Catch

In 1988 Paul Tavilla of Arlington, Mas-sachusetts, earned a place in the *Guin-ness World Records* by catching in his mouth a grape dropped from the top of New England's tallest skyscraper, the John Hancock Building, 788 feet from the top to Tavilla's tonsils.

When it comes to grape catching, what goes down obviously also goes up. The longest distance a grape has been caught after being thrown into the air from ground level is 99.82 meters—precisely 327 feet, 6 inches. That great grape catch was accomplished on May 27, 1991, by (who else?) Paul Tavilla. As a young boy, Tavilla learned to catch grapes and slices of fruit while working at his family's produce stand. His relatives would pass the time by tossing him things he'd catch in his mouth. Thankfully, no one ever flipped him a watermelon. For Tavilla's tips on how to catch a grape in your mouth, check out his Web site: www.thegrapecatcher.com.

* *

Boston Is Planet Hollywood
Boston University

Boston University is home to the largest collection of Hollywood memorabilia on the planet. The university's Department of Special Collections includes the personal papers and effects of some two thousand luminaries of the stage and silver screen. Included in the twentieth-century archive are materials from Mary Astor, Douglas Fairbanks Jr., Marilyn Monroe, Rex Harrison, Robert Redford, and Edward G. Robinson. The Oscar that Gene Kelly won for *An American in Paris* is on view, as are Fred Astaire's dancing shoes and Elizabeth Taylor's gloves.

Howard Gottlieb, curator of BU's Department of Special Collections, began going through the attics and shoe boxes of the stars in 1963. His most prized catch is 119,000 pages of material from Bette Davis. Gottlieb called Davis twice a week for thirty years before she agreed to donate her scripts, scrapbooks, and 5,000-volume library specializing in theater history.

In all, the archives take up 7 miles of shelves in two underground vaults. The Department of Special Collections is at 771 Commonwealth Avenue, fifth floor. Call ahead at (617) 353-3916 if you want to see something special.

The Boston University Bridge

Bostonians will tell you that the Boston University Bridge crossing the Charles River is the only bridge in the United States where an airplane can fly over a person riding a bicycle, next to a car, going over a train, that's traveling over a boat. It's true—that is, if you don't count the Brooklyn Bridge, where the train (a subway in a tunnel) goes under the boat.

The Iceman Stayeth
Boston University

Boston University dormitory Shelton Hall has, by legend, an exemplary resident tutor: Eugene O'Neill. Make that the *ghost* of the great American playwright. According to various stories, strange things happen in the building. The elevators sometimes stop for no obvious reason on the fourth floor, called the Writers' Corridor. O'Neill actually died in the building when it was a hotel back in 1953—suite 401. (O'Neill was quoted as saying that he was born in a hotel room and would end up dying in one.) The lights on the floor are dimmer than any other part of the building, and multiple attempts to correct the problem have failed. A director of the building has reported that her phone would sometimes dial the number 4 on its own when she picked up the handset. Residents of room 419, formerly the suite of the Nobel Prize winner, have reported hearing knocks on the door, but no one was standing there when they opened it. Some students have said that writing came easily when they went to the floor, although none have reported finding themselves typing *Long Day's Journey into Night.* Although you'll be on the ground and won't see a ghost, you can at least glance at the building at 91 Bay State Road.

Poetic Site
Copley Square

Boston is no stranger to statues of literary figures or artists, with Samuel Eliot Morison on Commonwealth Avenue and Edward Everett Hale's likeness at the Charles Street Gate of the Public Garden, or the statue of John Singleton Copley in Copley Square. But how many statues of writers and artists are created by their own god-children? You can see one in the monument to Khalil Gibran. The Lebanese-American author of *The Prophet,* a series of essays that has been in print since 1923, grew up in Boston. His writing may be his best remembered work, but Gibran was also a noted artist. Apparently there is something artistic about the name, as his godson, also named Khalil Gibran, became an artist and created a bronze relief of his godfather as a young poet. The work sits between Trinity Church and the Boston Public Library. But this was hardly a one-off for the artist. He's responsible for pieces in Back Bay, the South End, at the Federal Court House, in the collection of the Boston Museum of Fine Arts, and outside the Maronite Church of Our Lady of the Cedars in Jamaica Plain. However, few of his subjects could have said, "I remember when you were just this tall."

Tortoise and Hare Sculptures
Copley Square

These sculptures of the fabled hare and the tortoise commemorate the one hundredth anniversary of the Boston Marathon. The finish

Slow but steady wins the race to this
monument to the Boston Marathon.

★ ★

line is near here (see "Finally Finished Line"), and the fable fits the place—after all, the origin of the marathon is Greek and so is Aesop's timeless parable.

The site and statues are a mismatch, though. The sculptures weren't supposed to be in Copley Square, and the route they took to get here was long and tortuous. Local sculptor Nancy Schön felt that Boston was getting all the attention, so she wanted to honor Hopkinton, the town 26 miles away where the race begins. Soon, Schön ran into political correctness. The town wouldn't let her make a statue of a man, a woman, or someone in a wheelchair, so Schön sculptured the two 400-pound parable critters. She couldn't find a corporation to finance a piece of public art that was to be installed in a small town, however, so the statues sat in her garage for seven years. Finally, a member of the Friends of Copley Square got involved. They found funding to make this patch of the square the tortoise and hare's home, and here they are.

The Oak Bar

Copley Square

The Oak Bar in the Fairmont Copley Plaza is a place where time seems to stand still. The magnificent wood-paneled room with its 30-foot-high ceiling is reminiscent of an 1890s' British officers' club in the Far East. It exudes the luxury of a bygone era and a time when money was no object. If you order the engagement martini, it better be no object. Priced at $12,750, the engagement martini is served on the "rock": A diamond ring is placed at the bottom of the glass. For that, you and your to-be also get dinner in the Oak Room restaurant and an overnight in one of the hotel's suites.

In the 1930s the bar also served up something unusual. In the middle was a skating rink under a dance floor. Years later the rink was replaced with a merry-go-round that turned around on the hour. The merry-go-round was hard to miss but, apparently, easy to lose. It was dismantled in the late 1970s, and no one has seen it since. To commemorate the hotel's eighty-fifth anniversary, a $10,000 reward was offered for pieces of the whimsical bar. No one ever came forward to claim the prize. Still, what goes around comes around at the historic Fairmont Copley Plaza, 138 St. James Avenue. Call (617) 267-5300 or visit www.fairmont.com/CopleyPlaza.

Catie, the Canine Ambassador

Copley Square

The elegant Fairmont Copley Plaza has gone to the dogs. In front of the luxurious hotel's opulent front door is a doghouse. It's home for Catie Copley, the hotel's canine concierge. Catie's main role is to accompany visitors on walks around the neighborhood. Guests can sign out for a time to take the black Labrador on a tour, but she's a

Even Catie Copley sometimes lies down on the job.

busy girl and is often booked a month in advance. Catie was trained as a Seeing Eye dog but turned to the hospitality field when she developed cataracts. Jim Carey, the hotel's veteran human concierge, takes Catie home with him most nights. Even though she has the run of the hotel's 5,000-square-foot lobby, she refuses to use her doghouse out front. Clearly, she has good taste. The Fairmont Copley Plaza is at 138 St. James Avenue. Call (617) 267-5300 or visit www.fairmont.com/CopleyPlaza.

Finding a Lucky Lion's Tail and the Holy Grail
Copley Square

Bostonians simply call the Boston Public Library the BPL. It was the first free public lending library in the United States, and today, the building modeled after a classic Italian Renaissance palace, is a National Historic Landmark and the largest municipal library in the country.

The head of Minerva, the goddess of wisdom, is carved in the central keystone, and above her, check out the anatomically correct figures holding a shield. It's an open book inscribed with the library's motto "Free for All."

Designed by the architect Charles McKim, the building features the names of nineteenth-century writers, scientists, artists, and philosophers chiseled into the facade. It's said that McKim tried to have his name placed among those honored in stone, but the plan was detected before it was made permanent.

The McKim Building is as much a museum as a library. There are thirty-four million items here, including George Washington's Congressional Medal of Honor, the very first book ever published in the colonies, and the 3,800-volume personal library of John Adams.

As you enter, the ceiling is vaulted with domes in the side bays and the floor inlaid with brass symbols of the zodiac. Architect McKim went to Italy and personally selected each piece of marble you see here. Look closely at the grand staircase, and you'll find fossils

★ ★

Read between the lions at the BPL
and rub their tails for good luck.

embedded in the stone. At the top of the stairs is a pair of sculpted
lions. It's said that if you rub their tails, you get a day of good luck.

On the third floor are the famous John Singer Sargent murals,
considered America's Sistine Chapel. In the Abbey Room you'll see a
mural dedicated to the Holy Grail. The magnificent Bates Hall, named
for the library's first benefactor, is huge: 218 feet long, 42 feet wide,
and 50 feet high. The BPL is open seven days a week; volunteers offer
guided tours, and admission is, of course, free for all. Good luck!

Dancing Bacchante and Infant Faun

Copley Square

Located dead center in the courtyard of the Boston Public Library is
a statue that had been banned in Boston for a century. The work
by Frederick MacMonnies is called *Bacchante and Infant Faun* and

★ ★

features an exuberant nude young woman holding a bunch of grapes in one hand and a nude baby in the crook of her elbow. The artist gave the sculpture to the library's architect, Charles McKim, in appreciation of a $50 loan that had helped MacMonnies study sculpture in Beaux-Arts, Paris.

Prime and proper Brahmin Bostonians went bananas. The statue was nude! She had a baby but no wedding ring! Worse yet, she was tempting the infant with a bunch of grapes, which could only symbolize one thing! The masses wanted the wanton, bare-assed woman banished.

The terrified library trustees allowed the statue to be displayed in public for a brief period and then had her removed. The shameless statue quickly found a place of honor in New York City's Metropolitan

Bacchante upholds baby but not Boston morals.

Museum. In 1993, to commemorate the one hundredth anniversary of the museum, a bronze replica of *Bacchante* was unabashedly installed in the courtyard of the BPL, 700 Boylston Street.

The Sacco and Vanzetti Death Masks

Copley Square

There are many proud moments in Massachusetts's history, but August 23, 1927, is not one of them. That was the day when Italian immigrants Nicola Sacco, a shoemaker from Stoughton, and Bartolo-meo Vanzetti, a fisherman from North Plymouth, were executed on the site that is now part of Bunker Hill Community College in Boston. The men, followers of Italy's most radical anarchist, were found guilty of armed robbery and murder. Both denied the charges up to their deaths. The evidence against them was weak and circumstantial, and their executions ignited protests around the world. The case became a landmark in the judicial history of the state and nation. Fifty years to the day of their execution, then-governor Michael Dukakis issued a proclamation apologizing to the men and their families.

Copies of Sacco's and Vanzetti's death certificates are housed in the rare books department of the Boston Public Library, along with a canister of their ashes, their death masks, a box of bullets, and other personal items. BPL is at Copley Square. Visitors are asked to e-mail ahead of time so that the materials can be accessed. Write to rzonghi@bpl.org. The Boston Public Library's special collections also contain more than seven hundred anarchist newspapers and periodi-cals from around the world.

The Elephant in Pajamas

Copley Square

One of Boston's most distinctive shopping places is Copley Place Mall. You'll find it just two blocks from the square just south of the Boston Public Library. Or maybe you won't find it. The Boston historian David Wieneke has dubbed the place "the elephant in pajamas" because

Copley Place Mall hides in plain sight like an elephant in pajamas.

not only is it the largest real estate development in New England, but hidden and out of sight are four office buildings, two hotels, and a 2,000-space parking lot. "It's basically made to be an invisible piece of the city," says Wieneke, "because it's impossible to compete with the architecture around it. It's an elephant in pajamas!" What you don't see is what you get.

Rascal Kings Present
Copley Square

The Lenox Hotel in Copley Square was built in 1900 by Lucius Boomer, the owner of the Waldorf-Astoria in New York City. At the time, The Lenox was the tallest building in Boston, and over the years it has hosted royal visitors, stars, and even the son of a scoundrel. You can still see evidence of the scoundrel's son on display.

When Roger Saunders purchased The Lenox in 1963, he found, in the basement, two oval portraits wrapped in tablecloths. The portraits were of George and Martha Washington and had tags from the hotel's left luggage room.

As Saunders tells the story, he had the portraits hung in the hotel lobby when one day Connie Samson, a waiter who had worked at the Lenox for fifty years, asked Saunders if he knew the history behind the portraits.

It seems that, twenty years earlier, the paintings were left at the hotel by George Curley, son of Boston's "Rascal King," James Michael Curley. The elder Curley was colorful and corrupt. He served four terms in the U.S. Congress, one term as governor, and four terms as mayor of Boston. A two-time felon, at one point Curley ran the city from a cell in a federal penitentiary. When he was paroled the second time, the Rascal King went back to serving as mayor. One day an elegantly dressed woman with a butler visited Curley in his office at Old City Hall and presented the mayor with the two oval portraits of Martha and George.

Curley, ever a charmer, accepted the present, saying, "Madame, I'm just honored to receive them, and they will hang here in City Hall." The woman replied, "I just wanted to remind you of the honesty of your forefathers." When the lady left, the outraged mayor called his son, George, and said, "Get these paintings out of here. They're an insult to me."

George kept the paintings in his home in nearby Jamaica Plain, but when he fell on hard times, he sold the house, keeping only the paintings and his clothes, and moved into The Lenox. Months later he could not pay his hotel bill and had to go, leaving behind the paintings of George and Martha as collateral. There they stayed until Roger Saunders found them two decades later.

Today, the oval portraits of George and Martha Washington can be found in a second-floor function room. Roger Saunders had the

plaque engraved "Gift from James Michael Curley to the Lenox Hotel." The Lenox is at 61 Exeter Street. Call (617) 536-5300 or visit www.lenoxhotel.com.

All Washed Down

Copley Square

Trinity Church is an architectural marvel. Named by the American Institute of Architects as one of the ten greatest public buildings in the United States, it only takes a glance to see why. Part of it may be its neighbors, which offer a comparatively banal backdrop to its heavy grace and decoration. Its style is called Richardson Romanesque, for the particular approach that the architect Henry Hobson Richardson took on the stylistic marriage of Roman and Byzantine building, incorporating French and Spanish influences. But you only get the full effect when you walk into the church to see the magnificent stained-glass windows and 21,500 square feet of murals.

Even when it was built from 1872 to 1877, the church faced problems. Spongy ground, the heir of the landfill that provided a surface for construction, wouldn't take the weight that a taller tower would have required, so plans were made accordingly, and the tower was kept shorter than might otherwise have been expected. To support the tower, a 90-square-foot area was driven with over two thousand wooden piles. One problem facing the construction was all the water. Wood pilings kept wet are fine; it is only when they dry out that they rot and weaken. To avoid having these pilings dry out, they were deliberately cut 6 inches shorter than the other two thousand pilings elsewhere in the building. On top of the tower pilings were four massive granite pyramids. So long as the wood remained wet, the building was safe. But to make sure all remains well, so to speak, experts periodically drop a rope to measure how high the water level is. Hopefully, they won't have to install a tap. Trinity Church is at 206 Clarendon Street. Call (617) 536-0944 or visit www.trinitychurch boston.org for information.

Red Sox, Red Seat

Fenway

Boston's crown jewel, Fenway Park, is the oldest stadium in Major League Baseball. The first season was in 1912, and since then, the ballpark has been steeped in history and tradition. In left field is the Green Monster: Built in 1937, the 37-foot-high wall was painted green in 1947 to cover ads that graced the outfield fence. Fenway has

A red seat marks the spot where Ted Williams blasted his record-setting homer.

121

★ ★

the lowest seating capacity in the majors, and except for one in the right field, bleachers are painted green. Seat 21 in row 37 of section 42 is red. This is where, on June 9, 1946, Sox slugger Ted Williams hit the longest homer in Fenway history, a 502-foot blast that bonked a snoozing fan, Joseph Boucher, on the noggin. Serves him right; turns out Boucher was a Yankee fan. Fenway Park is located off Kenmore Square at 4 Yawkey Way.

Curiosity of the Month

Fenway

When Jeremy Belknap founded the Massachusetts Historical Society in 1791, he asked the public to submit unusual contributions to the organization's collection. Since then, the society's "curiosity collection" has grown to hold some very unusual artifacts, including a $5 bill featuring Santa Claus, issued in 1850 by the Howard Banking Company (it was legal tender back then); a letter from Boston native Benjamin Franklin describing his attempt to electrocute a turkey; tea from the Boston Tea Party; and a World Series medal from the 1912 Boston Red Sox. Little is known about the medal, but it is obviously very rare. After 1918 the Red Sox did not win the World Series again until 2004, finally overcoming the championship drought attributed to "the curse of the Bambino," when the Sox traded Babe Ruth to Boston's archrival, the New York Yankees. The Massachusetts Historical Society is at 1154 Boylston Street. Call (617) 536-1608. The society maintains an "object of the month" online showcase of some of its more unusual artifacts at www.masshist.org/welcome.

What You Don't See Is What You Used to Get

Fenway

The magnificent Isabella Stewart Gardner Museum boasts an eclectic collection of more than 2,500 paintings, sculptures, tapestries, pieces of furniture, manuscripts, and rare books. Mrs. Gardner, the grande dame of Boston's Brahmin high society, spent thirty years assembling the renowned collection and built a fifteenth-century Venetian palace with courtyard garden to house it.

But today what makes the collection a must-see for many tourists is what you don't see, as evidenced by the empty frames that hang on the walls. On St. Patrick's Day 1990, the Gardner Museum was the scene of the biggest art heist in U.S. history. Two men wearing fake mustaches and Boston police uniforms stole thirteen priceless works of art. Among them were three Rembrandts (including the master's only seascape), five Degas sketches, a Manet, and Vermeer's *Concert.* Despite a $5 million reward, none of the pieces has been recovered. The empty frames continue to hang on the walls because Mrs. Gardner stipulated in her will that everything in the house was forever to remain exactly as it was, or all her possessions would pass to Harvard University. The FBI still has an active investigation, but because the statute of limitations ran out after twelve years, the thieves could be free of prosecution.

The Isabella Stewart Gardner Museum is located at 280 The Fenway. For more information, call (617) 566-1401, or visit www .gardnermuseum.org. The Gardner is closed on most major holidays and usually on St. Patrick's Day.

Lasting Victory
Fenway

In this country, World War II meant privations of various sorts, especially food. Rationing was necessary because the United States had to export so much food to troops fighting in Europe. To help ease the burden, victory gardens became popular. People transformed small open plots of land into vegetable gardens at the behest of President Franklin Delano Roosevelt. Boston established forty-nine of these areas in spaces that included such park areas as Boston Common, the Public Garden, and the Back Bay Fens. Eventually, the Allies won, and the need for supplemental gardening became a historic relic. But one garden remained: the

★ ★

Richard D. Parker Memorial Victory Gardens, named in honor of one of the original organizations but usually called the Fenway Victory Gardens. Its seven acres are still actively run by the Fenway Garden Society. There are more than five hundred plots, each measuring roughly 15 by 25 feet. People have to join a waiting list for their turn to plant a plot. There are annual events, or you can drop by during the growing season and stroll about the grounds. Just plant yourself in the green area between Boylston Street to the north, Agassiz Road to the south, the Fenway on the east, and Park Drive on the west. The main entrance is at the corner of Boylston and Park. If you're interested in scoping out the area in advance or need some urban gardening tips, you can also have your browser look up www.fenwayvictorygardens.com.

Ringing the Bell
Fenway

The greater Boston area seems to have an affinity for picking up bells that have been lying around on scrap heaps. Cambridge had its Russian monastery bells rescued and brought back to Harvard (and ultimately returned and replaced, as we mention in "The Russian Belle Bells"). But Boston was also the recipient of an intervention. A Japanese temple bell, cast in 1675 by Tanaka Gonzaemon under the supervision of Suzuki Magoemon, had been contributed to the Japanese government in 1940 as part of its World War II effort. But for some reason, the bell ended up sitting in Yokosuka, a city on Tokyo Bay, waiting to be turned into scrap. A group of sailors from the USS *Boston* snagged it after World War II in 1945 and brought it back to the ship's namesake. Eight years later, Japan made it an official gift to the city of Boston in the name of peace. People refer to it as one of the oldest works of public art in Boston, but given its date, we can't think of a single competitor for the title of most venerated. You can find the Japanese Temple Bell right near another pleasant stop: the James P. Kelleher Rose Garden, whose two hundred varieties of roses are off Park Drive, just a little north of Agassiz Road.

Here's to You, Kid

Fenway

Forget about the recent steroid-fueled poseurs and their baseball-hitting records. A real contender for the greatest hitter of all time was Red Sox legend Ted Williams, also known as The Kid, the Splendid Splinter, Teddy Ballgame, and The Thumper. When it came to batting, Williams was a phenomenon. His career batting average was .344, he was the last major league player to break a .400 average (.406) in a season, and he had a career 521 home runs. He also holds the record for reaching base in the most consecutive games (eighty-four). In two separate seasons he won the game's Triple Crown, leading the league in home runs, runs batted in, and batting average, and he was twice named the American League's most valuable player. His devotion to the art of hitting was famous, and in 1970 he wrote *The Science of Hitting,* which is still a de rigueur read for players. And he managed his success while taking time off to be a pilot in World War II and the Korean War, although the conflicts occurred during his prime years. Williams has passed on, but you can see a statue honoring him just outside Fenway Park near the corner of Van Ness and Ipswich Streets.

This Sign Is a Gas

Kenmore Square

Soaring 200 feet high over Kenmore Square, seemingly floating in midair, is one of Boston's more obvious and beloved landmarks: the Citgo sign. Built by City Services Oil Company in 1965, the giant ad measures 60 by 60 feet. Originally, the two-sided sign was lit with 5,878 orange, red, and white neon tubes. In 2005 they were replaced with more efficient LEDs.

Appropriately enough, the brightly lit sign is located on Beacon Street and is used by Bostonians to orient themselves around the city. However, in 1973 residents wandered around confused and directionless when the lights were turned off for a year as a symbol of conservation during the energy crisis. Then from 1979 to 1982 there

★ ★

It's hard to take a dim view of this Boston icon.

were again lost souls in the streets when the sign was turned off once more to save electricity.

Just how important the Citgo sign had become to residents became clear in November 1982, when workers arrived to dismantle the sign. Before they could remove a single bulb, the Boston Landmarks Commission intervened, saying the sign was a "prime example of roadside culture." There was talk of designating the sign an official city landmark, but Citgo would have had to pay to move it. Instead, the company paid $450,000 to refurbish the sign and return it to its original glow. On August 10, 1983, as the song "You Light Up My Life" filled the air in Kenmore Square, 750 people attended the relighting ceremony.

The sign has not been without controversy. In 2006 a Boston City Council member proposed removing the icon because Citgo is owned by the Venezuelan government, whose president, Hugo Chavez, insulted then president George W. Bush. Nothing became of the effort. The Citgo sign still shines proudly over the square.

The Massachusetts Vikings
Kenmore Square

Three public monuments in eastern Massachusetts claim that it was the Viking Leif Eriksson in 1000, not Christopher Columbus in 1492, who was the first European to set foot on North America. The monuments were built by Eben Norton Horsford, a Harvard professor of chemistry turned amateur archaeologist who was convinced that "Leif the Lucky" was the first European in the New World.

Professor Horsford made a fortune in the mid-nineteenth century selling Horsford's Cream of Tartar Substitute, a new-formula baking powder, and used the money to fund excavations in Cambridge, Weston, and Watertown, Massachusetts. According to Horsford, Eriksson landed on Cape Cod, sailed up the Charles River, and built a house in what is now Cambridge. Horsford said he found some buried Norse artifacts near the intersection of Memorial Drive, Mount Auburn Street, and Gerry's Landing Road. He built a small monument there marking the spot.

Farther upstream stands Norumbega Tower. Horsford built the structure in 1889 to commemorate the site on which he believed the Vikings had constructed the legendary Norse settlement of the same name. A summary of Horsford's theory is engraved on a plaque on the tower. To see it, take Route 128 to Route 30 West to River Road North.

The third monument to Horsford's fanciful theory is located at Charlesgate East on Commonwealth Avenue, near Kenmore Square in Boston. It was unveiled in 1887 and depicts Leif the Lucky on a pedestal scanning the distant horizon. The back of the memorial is inscribed: LEIF THE DISCOVERER SON OF ERIK WHO SAILED FROM ICELAND AND LANDED ON THIS CONTINENT AD 1000.

Leif the Lucky strikes a pose on Commonwealth
Avenue in Kenmore Square.

Horsford's theories of Vikings in Cambridge were later debunked
as just bunk, and he's considered a crackpot today. But recent scientific analysis of a controversial parchment drawing, the so-called
Vinland Map, and an accompanying manuscript called "The Tartar
Relation" seem to suggest that maybe the chemist was onto something archaeological after all.

5

Boston Burbs

Boston doesn't have *all the fun. A little traveling around the edge of the hub of the universe, and you'll find the first public outdoor swimming pool in the United States, the country's oldest automobile collection, a bridge measured in smoots, the largest collection of slide rules, Click and Clack's office, the statue of John Harvard that isn't John Harvard, glass flowers, and a museum of bad art. You might learn that the song "Jingle Bells" wasn't written about Christmas and find the home of Fluff. There's a castle of humor, a place you can find Buckminster Fuller and Fanny Farmer, and even a Boston park that is 17 miles outside the city limits. There's also a time capsule that no one can reach . . . because it's sitting under an 18-ton magnet.*

★ ★

A Well-Done Museum
Arlington

Where there's smoke, there's Deborah Henson-Conant. Put a harp in her hands, and, boy, can she cook! With her long beaded hair and leather halter top, she plays the heaven-sent instrument with the fire of a bat out of . . . well, you-know-where.

Doc Severinsen calls Henson-Conant a wild woman of the harp, serving up blues, jazz, Celtic, and folk music with a generous dash of humor. But put her in the kitchen of her Arlington, Massachusetts, home, and the menu changes dramatically. Henson-Conant is the founder of (and curator, and primary contributor to) the Museum

I had a **SMOKIN'** good time!

Free-Standing!
Hot Apple Cider
circa 1989

At The
MUSEUM of BURNT FOOD
www.BurntFoodMuseum.com
Celebrating nearly two decades
of Culinary Disaster

WARNING:
Official Field Research in Process

For a meal Smokey Bear might love, check out the Museum of Burnt Food.
Photo courtesy of Deborah Henson—Conant

✦ ✦

of Burnt Food, an ever-expanding collection that celebrates the art of culinary disaster. Sometime in 1989, while heating a pot of apple cider on her stove, she was distracted from her task by a lengthy telephone call. By the time she returned, the cider had turned to cinder (exhibit A). She proudly mounted and displayed the piece, and, voilà, the Museum of Burnt Food was born. The museum's motto: "To cook the museum way—always leave the flame on low . . . and then take a long nap."

There's nothing half-baked about this eccentric collection of fire-fossilized food. Over the years Henson-Conant has cooked up, entirely by accident, the Forever Shrimp Kebab; Well, Well Done Soy Pups; and Thrice-Baked Potatoes. The entire collection is on limited public display in Henson-Conant's home by invitation only, but it can be savored from a safe distance on line at www.burntfoodmuseum.com.

First One in the Water

Belmont

The first outdoor public swimming pool in America opened on June 17, 1912, in Belmont, Massachusetts. The pool was the idea of Belmont resident Henry Underwood (of Underwood Deviled Ham fame), who owned the property. Underwood felt children in the neighborhood weren't having as much fun as he had while growing up. He got the idea for a swimming hole because a natural spring near his property bubbled water to the surface.

Underwood's brother, Loring, a landscape architect, set out to design the pool but found that nothing like it had been done in the United States before. Today, the pool retains most of its original shape, although a stone island in the middle is long gone. The cement block bathhouse was built years later and designed by Henry Underwood's nephew. A large clock was installed over the doorway to "help the children keep in mind the hour for going home."

Go underwater at the Underwood Pool on Concord Avenue. You can't miss it. Just listen for the kids squealing with delight.

Brain Bank

The Scarecrow in *The Wizard of Oz* would have loved this place. It's the world's largest brain bank. Officially known as the Harvard Brain Tissue Resource Center, the warehouse holds more than four thousand brains. The brains were donated by individuals and used by medical researchers to study Alzheimer's disease, Parkinson's disease, schizophrenia, and other neurologic disorders. On average one new brain a day is added to the repository. Some parts are preserved in formaldehyde and stored in Tupperware containers; others are flash frozen. It's a permanent place to rest a weary mind. Deposits are a no-brainer. Anyone over the age of eighteen can simply complete the "Brain Donation Registration" form available online. Call ahead or check out www.brainbank.mclean.org.

"From knowledge will come a cure."

Harvard Brain Tissue Resource Center

1-800-BRAIN BANK

http://www.brainbank.mclean.org:8080

Marble and Mâché Man

Brookline

Bertram Cohen readily admits he's crazy about his hobby, but obviously he hasn't lost his marbles. In fact, at last count he had 300,000, constituting what he believes is the largest collection of marbles in the world. He's got onion skins, Joseph's coats, sulfides, immies, aggies, and, of course, cat's eyes.

Bert has been a marble consultant and historian for more than forty years, collecting, swapping, and selling marbles large and small, old and new online. His largest marble is a custom-made job that rolls in at 33 pounds; the smallest is just 1/16 inch in diameter. One of his most unusual and valuable marbles is 4,300 years old, which is kid stuff when you consider that the game goes back 10,000 years. Bert has clearly raised the collection to an art form; one marble Rembrandt played with has been authenticated by the Smithsonian Institution and the Corning Glass Museum.

Bert doesn't play anymore himself, but he does give out mass-produced marbles by the shovelful to worthy causes, such as the Boy Scouts. He gets them from a factory in Mexico that rolls out fifteen million a day. Collectors who share Bert's mania for marbles gather at an annual event he has organized for the past quarter century in—where else?—Marlborough, Massachusetts.

Now, having the world's most stupendous collection of marbles might be enough for some people, but Bert Cohen is a well-rounded collector. The self-described pack rat also has an extensive collection of glassware and recently donated to his son what must certainly be the largest, if not only, collection of toys made by the long-gone Irving Corporation, maker of some of the first plastic toys.

Bert also has one of the world's largest collections of objets de macerated money. From 1874 to 1942 officials at the U.S. Treasury Department decided that burning old paper currency was too dirty, so they turned it into pulp. At first, the Bureau of Engraving and Printing rolled the mushy paper into bookbinders, but an employee turned

★ ★

entrepreneur started making papier-mâché sculptures from the notes. Soon others were making everything from busts of George Washington, to shoes (made from a cool ten grand), to postcards from the stuff.

Bert recently packed up his buckets, bins, and barrels full of marbles and macerated money and moved from Boston to nearby Brookline, Massachusetts. Visits to Bertram Cohen's marble museum and toy emporium are by special invitation only, but you can learn more about his marbles at his Web site, www.marblebert.com/publications.htm.

In Their Merry Oldsmobile

From the outside, the building looks like someone tried to cross an English manor with a castle. But inside what was actually a carriage house, the Larz Anderson Car Museum houses the oldest automobile collection in the United States. The collection started with a purchase by the Andersons. Larz was with the State Department. Isabel Weld Perkins had grown up wealthy after inheriting $17 million from her grandfather when she was five years old. When the two married in 1897, they had money to spare and an eye for public service. Two years later, they bought their first car, an 1899 Winton 4-horsepower runabout, and on Sunday afternoons they would open their carriage house to visitors. From then through 1948, they bought at least thirty-two cars, creating the oldest motorcar collection in the United States. Eventually, the two left their estate to the town of Brookline as a sixty-four-acre park. In 1949 the carriage house opened as an automobile museum. If you'd like to see some of the cars, motor to 15 Newton Street, or check the Web site, www.larzanderson.org.

Uncomfortable at Any Fete

Only the president of Harvard University is allowed to sit in an uncomfortable three-legged chair, and then, only during the school's annual June commencement ceremony.

The chair, measuring about 4 feet high and 32 inches wide, is a "three-square" design made in England or Wales sometime in the sixteenth century. It's graced with knobby dowels and filials and was first used by Harvard's ninth president, Edward Holyoke. Holyoke was often asked about the chair but had no idea where it came from. Collectors say it's the only one of its kind in the United States. Oliver Wendell Holmes described it as a "funny old chair with a seat like a wedge, sharp behind and broad front edge."

At first it was used as just a piece of everyday furniture. Later on school lore has it that it was placed in Harvard Library, where, according to tradition, a student had permission to kiss any young woman who sat on it. These days that kind of thing would get you a seat at the witness table, and you'd wind up commencing to jail.

Eventually the chair is to be displayed in the Fogg Museum, which is being renovated and is not scheduled to reopen until 2013. Visit www.harvardartmuseum.org for current information.

Boston's Far Out Park

Burlington

Boston's twelfth-largest park is not located in Boston; it's 17 miles north, straddling the Burlington–Woburn line.

In her will, Mary Cummings bequeathed 210 acres of family farmland to the city of Boston with the provision that it be kept "the same forever open as a public pleasure ground, and to maintain and care for the same in a suitable manner in accordance with that purpose." But today, a group known as the Friends of Mary Cummings Park says it

is anything but a public pleasure. They charge Boston officials with neglecting the park, letting it fall into disrepair, and misappropriating funds that were supposed to be used to maintain the land. In early 2009 city workers demolished the only building in the park, declaring it a safety hazard. Boston officials have also considered selling the park but are prohibited under the terms of Mary Cummings's bequest. Seems where there's a will, there's no way.

During the cold war, the federal government seized the park by eminent domain and used it as a Nike missile site. Today it is used by a local model aircraft club. Mary Cummings Park is on Blanchard Road. For more information, check http://cummingspark.org.

Glad to Pay You Tuesday
Cambridge

The sign on the door reads, ON THIS SITE IN 1897 NOTHING HAPPENED, but sixty-three years later 1246 Massachusetts Avenue would forever be known more as Boston's landmark to burgerdom. It was in 1960 when Joe Bartley decided the world needed a best burger, and he's been serving them up ever since. It's not just Joe who says his 7-ounce beef patty is the planet's primo; so did *Gourmet* magazine, which named Mr. Bartley's Burger Cottage one of the top fifty restaurants in America, and so did the *Boston Globe,* which declared Mr. B's sliders "the best burgers in the world."

The inside decor is an eclectic mix of frat house funkiness, with the walls filled with visual delights, while one whiff from the grill tells you this is no ordinary burger joint. Mr. B's son, Bob Bartley, has been presiding over the grill for more than thirty years and is to the burger what Baryshnikov is to ballet. It's a virtuoso performance as Bob flips and stacks, fries and sautés in one fluid motion. How does he possibly keep track of the orders the waitstaff shout out? Be sure to grab a stool at the counter to catch his act. Meanwhile, Mrs. B manages the door, herding hamburger aficionados to their tables. If Harvard University, which is across the street, gave out degrees, this family would get PhD's in burgerology. Bartley's burgers are piled high and deep with homemade fixings and a hearty helping of tradition. Mr. Bartley's Burger Cottage is at 1246 Massachusetts Avenue. Call (617) 354-6559, or go to www.mrbartley.com for hours.

Joe and Joan Bartley in front of their Cambridge burger cottage landmark.

★ ★

Requiem for a Puppet Master
Cambridge

In 1993 Igor Fokin moved from St. Petersburg, Russia, to Cambridge with nothing but a box of hand-carved wood puppets, some string, and a dream. On a corner of Brattle Square in Cambridge, Fokin set up his sidewalk show, every quarter hour delighting locals and tourists with his marionettes. Fokin crafted each puppet by hand, sewing their costumes and painting their features. He once said that he carved the wood to let the character out and tied string to them so they wouldn't run away. Fokin was issued a special visa to live and work in the United States, which declared him "a person of extraordinary ability and talent." In 1996 Igor Fokin died suddenly. He was just thirty-six years old. Residents and other street performers dedicated a memorial to Fokin on September 22, 2001. The bronze statue features Doo Doo, one of Fokins most beloved characters. The Igor Fokin Memorial Sculpture is on the southeast corner of Brattle Square.

Beloved Doo Doo.

Hey, Citgo Sign, Clam Up!

Cambridge

Literally and figuratively sitting in the shadow of Boston's famous Citgo sign is one owned by competitor Shell Oil, just across the Charles River. Built in 1933 and in operation continuously ever since, the giant scallop-shell neon is one of two that were constructed for Shell's regional headquarters on Commonwealth Avenue in Boston. In 1944, possibly in response to wartime restrictions, the company removed the signs. One was dismantled; the surviving spectacular neon sign was relocated to the existing Shell gas station on Memorial Drive. The Cambridge Historical Commission deemed the sign an artifact of early commercial development in the city. The commission

Memorial Drive in Cambridge is home to the giant Shell Oil sign.

designated the Shell sign a historic and protected landmark, and in 1994 the sign was put on the National Register of Historic Places. The Shell sign is at the intersection of Magazine Street and Memorial Drive.

It's MIT by a Smoot

Cambridge

The techies who attend Massachusetts Institute of Technology (MIT) deal with precise standard units of measure: the angstrom, the meter, the light-year, and the smoot. The latter, while perhaps unfamiliar to laypeople, is an exacting measure: precisely 5 feet, 7 inches.

There are just two things in the known universe measured in smoots: the Harvard Bridge connecting the MIT campus in Cambridge to Boston's Back Bay (364.4 smoots plus one ear) and Oliver R. Smoot Jr., MIT class of '62 (one smoot).

In October 1958, when O. R. Smoot Jr. was an MIT freshman pledge to the Lambda Chi Alpha fraternity, a fraternity brother decided it would be useful if students walking back to campus from Boston during the fog and snow knew how much farther they had to walk. Smoot, the smallest of the pledges, was measured with a string, and the unit known as the smoot was born. The fraternity members marked off the smoots in paint on the bridge. When a police van appeared at about the 300-smoot mark, the measurers took off, returning later to finish the job.

Today the pledge class of Lambda Chi Alpha repaints the smoots with a new color twice a year, and the police are no longer a problem. In fact, officers use the markers to indicate locations on the bridge when writing up accident reports. To make matters easier, the Continental Construction Company of Cambridge now makes concrete sidewalk slabs 5 feet, 7 inches long to coincide with the smoots, instead of the usual 6-foot increments.

Ironically, in 2005, Oliver Smoot retired as chairman of the American National Standards Institute. The organization sets standard units and measurement guidelines.

★ ★

Oliver Smoot repainting smoots.

You can count the smoots yourself by walking over the Harvard Bridge from Massachusetts Avenue in Cambridge to Boston. (By the way, MIT calls the span the Harvard Bridge, even though it is located next to the MIT campus. The school considered it an example of inferior engineering and gave the dubious honor to its archrival, that small liberal arts college down Massachusetts Avenue.)

It Makes War and Peace Look like a Skirmish
Cambridge

If you wanted to snuggle up for a little bedtime reading with the book *Bhutan: A Visual Odyssey across the Last Himalayan Kingdom,*

you'd better have a very big bed. Actually, the book is so big, it could be your bed. According to the *Guinness World Records,* the 114-page tome is the largest commercial book ever published. It is 5 feet high, opens to nearly 7 feet wide, and weighs more than 130 pounds. Two gallons of ink are needed to print a single book, each of which costs $10,000. Most of the proceeds go to charity, to send students from Bhutan abroad to study.

The hefty read is the creation of Michael Hawley, the director of special projects at the Massachusetts Institute of Technology. Hawley was inspired by numerous trips to the remote Shangri-la kingdom. He also wanted to demonstrate state-of-the art publishing technology.

Bhutan's leaders have charted a unique course for their country. The government's stated economic plan is to achieve the highest level

Tee for Too-th

Harvard University dentist George Grant is known internationally for his invention of the oblate palate, a device used to help people with cleft palate. Never heard of it? Well, how about Dr. Grant's other invention, the wooden golf tee?

Until 1899, when Dr. G came along with his tee, duffers carried buckets of sand to each hole, building up a pyramid-shaped mound that they could set their ball upon.

Dr. Grant received U.S. Patent No. 638,920 for his invention and the eternal gratitude of greens maintenance crews. But he never mass produced his tees or made a penny from his invention. Instead, he had them manufactured by a local company and then gave them away to friends and fellow golfers.

George Franklin Grant was the son of a former slave, the first African American awarded a scholarship to attend Harvard's Dental School, and the university's first black faculty member.

of "gross national happiness." Television was not even allowed into the country until 1999, no doubt because the Bhutanese are very big readers.

The Acme Bookbinding Company in Charlestown, Massachusetts, is the exclusive source of *Bhutan: A Visual Odyssey across the Last Himalayan Kingdom.* Acme calls itself not only the world's oldest book-bindery, but also the world's largest bookbindery. Acme has more information about the big book on its Web site, www.acmebook.com.

Michael Hawley, publisher and author of *Bhutan: A Visual Odyssey across the Last Himalayan Kingdom,* standing next to the world's largest published book at Acme Bookbinding Company, where the books are made.

For Solving Really Big Problems

Cambridge

It's only fitting and proper that MIT is the home to one of the world's largest collections of that icon of pretransistor engineering, the slide rule.

In 2005, after months of intense negotiations, the MIT museum became the permanent repository of the Keuffel & Esser Company Slide Rule Collection. The New Jersey firm was the largest producer of the antiquated calculators in the United States. Among the more than six hundred historic slip slicks are a rare three-sided brass rule and giant 2.5-meter-long models used for demonstration purposes. The curator of the MIT Museum, Deborah Douglas, calls the slide rule the most important technology of the twentieth century that historians

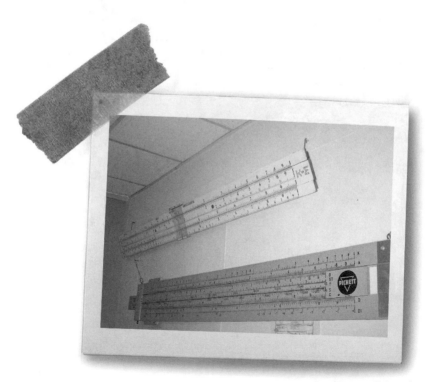

Only at MIT does one make an appointment to see a slide rule.

have not studied yet. Not far from the museum, MIT engineers used slide rules to design the first lunar lander.

The slide rule collection is currently housed in the basement of the museum at 265 Massachusetts Avenue and can be seen by special appointment. Bring a pocket protector, and you'll fit right in. For further information, call (617) 253-4444, or visit http://web.mit.edu/museum.

Who Said Grime Doesn't Pay?

Cambridge

Since 1977 Elizabeth Magliozzi's sons have been driving radio listeners nuts and sending them reaching for their dials. Her boys, Tom and Ray, better known as Click and Clack of the weekly show *Car*

Car Talk Plaza, appropriately located above the Curious George shop in Harvard Square, is the intergalactic headquarters of public radio grease monkeys Click and Clack.

★ ★

Talk, are a public-radio phenomenon. These days they have two million listeners a week, from Sweden to Sheboygan. The gregarious grease monkeys are a mega-industry, perpetually trying to unload their books, records, T-shirts, and whatever else they can get away with on their shameless e-commerce Web site. The entire shenanigans come out of *Car Talk*'s dumpy offices high above Harvard Square in Cambridge, aka "our fair city," and can be found above the Curious George store at the intersection of Massachusetts Avenue and JFK Street. To learn more about what Click and Clack call "our lousy radio show," check out their Web site, www.cartalk.com. Whatever you do, don't drive like these brothers.

The Thais That Bind
Cambridge

In Cambridge, at an intersection at the edge of Brattle Square (which is actually just an intersection on the edge of Harvard Square), you will find yet another square with a curious name. King Bhumibol Adulyadej Square commemorates the reign of the only monarch born on American soil. His Majesty, King Bhumibol of Thailand, was born at Mount Auburn Hospital in Cambridge in 1927 while his parents studied medicine at Harvard.

King Bhumibol ascended to the Thai throne in 1946, and in 2000 he became the longest-reigning ruler in the world. He is also the only reigning monarch ever to win a gold medal—or any medal, for that matter—at an international sporting event. He won a medal for sailing in the Southeast Asian Peninsular Games. The king was also the first member of a royal family ever to receive a patent. In 2003 he received his fourth patent, for inventing an artificial rainmaking technique.

According to the 2009 *Forbes'* list of the world's richest royals, King Bhumibol took top honors with an estimated wealth of $30 billion. A photograph of the king can be found next to the elevators on the maternity floor at Mount Auburn Hospital. If you want to learn

Photos in the maternity ward at Mount Auburn Hospital
honor the only king born in the United States.

more about the Cambridge–Thailand connection, ask for Joe at the
Union Oyster House in Boston (941 Union Street; www.unionoyster
house.com). In addition to being the owner of the restaurant, Joe
Milano is honorary consul of Thailand.

Harvard University's Famous Overachieving Nongrads
Cambridge

Some of the most distinguished people in the world have earned
diplomas from Harvard University, including eight U.S. presidents,
poet T. S. Eliot, authors Norman Mailer and John Updike, educator W.
E. B. DuBois, jurist Oliver Wendell Holmes, Senator Elizabeth Dole, and
many more household names.

★ ★

And then there is the list of equally distinguished Harvard students who walked the same hallowed halls but never graduated. Among those who dropped out of Harvard or were otherwise "excused" are actor Matt Damon; poets Robert Lowell, Robert Frost, and Ogden Nash; and Edwin Land, the inventor of the Polaroid camera and holder of more than five hundred patents. R. Buckminster Fuller dropped out twice—once during midterms so he could take a dancer and her entire chorus to dinner. William Randolph Hearst got the boot after sending personally inscribed chamber pots to his professors while they were considering his academic probation, and bazillionaire Bill Gates left Harvard in his junior year to devote his energies to his fledgling start-up, Microsoft. Thirty years later he received an honorary doctorate from the university.

Pop singer Bonnie Raitt never made it through. Neither did folk singer Pete Seeger, although he was honored years later with the Harvard Arts Medal, telling the crowd that he "was tempted to accept [it] on behalf of all Harvard dropouts."

The Archive of Useless Research
Cambridge

At last count, there were fifty-six current or former members of the MIT community who had won a Nobel Prize. MIT is a center of superb scholarship, intellectual excellence, innovative entrepreneurship, and some of the craziest, crackpot pseudoscientific research you will ever find in one place. In room 14N–118 of the Hayden Library's Special Collections, collection number MC 187 consists of six large boxes known as MIT's Archive of Useless Research. It's a reminder that sometimes scientific exploration respects no boundaries, even when it should.

The archive began at MIT's Engineering Library as "the American Institute of Useless Research," a collection of crank files sent to the school's researchers over the years. In 1940 Albert Ingalls, an editor of *Scientific American,* began adding useless but invaluable research that had come his way, and the institute morphed into today's current

★ ★

archive. Although the archive stopped adding to the collection in 1965, it certainly was not for lack of ongoing kooky research.

The collection is a celebration of screwball science, unpublished articles, self-published books, and rejected theories sent to MIT researchers over the years and deemed deserving of preservation for posterity. Included are such breakthrough studies as "Darwin as a Pirate" and "The Riddle of the Universe Solved." The archive can be seen at the Hayden Library, 160 Memorial Drive, Cambridge. The archivist suggests you call ahead (617-253-5690) so they can retrieve this fascinating collection in advance of your visit. Bring your aluminum foil helmet.

Hasty, Not Tasty, Pudding

Harvard University's Hasty Pudding Club was founded in 1790 as a secret social society. The club is named for a traditional American porridge made with milk and corn, which is required to be served at every meeting. Membership in the Pudding is selective and includes five U.S. presidents (John Adams, John Quincy Adams, Teddy Roosevelt, FDR, and JFK). In 1881 the club formed the Hasty Pudding Theatricals, which today is the nation's oldest theater company. For the past few decades male members of the organization have dressed up in drag and awarded man and woman of the year awards—a Hasty Pudding Pot. Recipient John Wayne showed up in Harvard Square in an M-113 armored personnel carrier. Other winners of the pot are John Travolta, Bob Hope, and Samuel L. Jackson. Female winners include Katharine Hepburn, Mamie Eisenhower, Jane Fonda, and Cher. Hasty pudding has played a role in the school's history from the very start. Harvard College's first schoolmaster, who was eventually fired for allegedly beating one of his students, had a wife who reportedly served students pudding with goat dung in it.

★ ★

It's Kismet, the Robo Sapien

Cambridge

Kismet is a moody infant, one minute sad, the next happy; a few seconds later, angry; then calm, bored, or surprised. If Kismet were a baby with colic, you could understand, but Kismet isn't a baby. Kismet is a robot—more accurately, a 7-pound robot head. Still, that is enough to land Kismet in the *Guinness World Records* for being the most emotionally responsive robot ever built.

Created by Dr. Cynthia Breazeal at the Massachusetts Institute of Technology, Kismet has movable facial features that can express basic human emotions, as well as electronic eyes and ears to interact with its environment and people. If you stop playing with Kismet, it acts bored; shake a doll in front of the dismembered head, and it looks

Kismet is all eyes, ears, and emotions.

agitated. Kismet's gremlinlike features are powered by twenty-one motors and fifteen huge computers.

It's a good thing that Kismet has been retired to the MIT Museum, or it would have the look of envy that comes with sibling rivalry. Back in the lab, Kismet has a big brother, COG, a 7-foot-tall artificial humanoid with arms, hands, a sense of touch, and the ability to talk. To make COG even more humanlike, researchers are working on a biochemical system to run it. Ultimately, it is hoped that COG will have the intelligence equivalence of a two-year-old child.

It's the stuff of science fiction, complete with profound philosophical implications. Of course, there are also practical concerns. Perhaps robo-researchers will know they have gone too far when the machines they create in their own image start asking for the car keys. You can see Kismet and videos of it interacting with its creator at the MIT Museum, 265 Massachusetts Avenue. For more information, check out the museum's Web site, http://web.mit.edu/museum, or call (617) 253-4444.

MIT Eager Beavers Reach for the Brass Rat
Cambridge

Graduates of the Massachusetts Institute of Technology receive a special badge of honor and symbol of intellectual distinction and achievement for studying day and night, sweating through brain-bending tests, and ruining their social lives. It's the Brass Rat. That's the name affectionately bestowed on MIT's class ring, which, since 1930, has featured the MIT mascot, the beaver. After all, like MIT students, beavers are nocturnal, industrious, and master builders, but on the ring, the beaver, which is an aquatic rodent, looks like a rat. Hence the nickname.

The design changes each year, created by a committee from each class that spends the better part of a year meeting in secret. By tradition, the design contains the letters *IHTFP*, an acronym with a number of interpretations underscoring the love–hate relationship

By tradition, the Brass Rat contains secret codes and symbols. In this design, hidden in the waves of the Charles River along the MIT campus, are the letters A=B=C=P, representing the fact that the class of 2005 was the last to have pass/no record in their entire freshman year. Notice the hand of the student drowning in the river. The ZZZ to the right of the beaver's tail is for the constant attention to the student's lack of sleep. See if you can find the letters IHTFP

Photo Courtesy of MIT

MIT students have with their school. Some say it means "I Have Truly Found Perfection." Others say it stands for "I Hate This !$@#% Place." Both camps proudly wear the Brass Rat; nearly 95 percent of the student body buys one.

Another tradition is the way the students wear their rings, which they purchase in their sophomore year. As undergraduates, the bottom of the beaver faces in toward the student; at the graduation ceremony, the class en masse removes the rings and turns them the other way. The saying is that while they are students, the beaver excretes on them, but after they graduate, it excretes on the world.

Truth Be Told, Harvard's Statue Is a Liar
Cambridge

For a university whose motto is "Veritas," you would expect the truth, the whole truth, and nothing but the truth. But check out the statue of the venerable school's namesake, John Harvard, standing right in front of University Hall. It's a pack of lies. In fact, it is called the "Statue of Three Lies." The inscription beneath the statue reads: JOHN HARVARD, FOUNDER, 1638. Not a word of it is true.

The college (it was a college back then) was founded in 1636 by the Massachusetts Bay Colony in what was then the village of New-towne, which later became Cambridge. John Harvard was an early benefactor to the college; he was its first professor, erected Harvard's first building, and planted its first apple orchard. One thing John

The "Statue of Three Lies" stands (or sits) in Harvard Yard.

★ ★

Harvard wasn't was the founder. The college was named for him in 1639 after he donated his library to the school. Nor is the statue a likeness of John Harvard. There were no pictures or images of him, so the sculptor, Daniel Chester French, chose a student at random as his model and dressed him in seventeenth-century garb.

And truth be told, the statue actually contains four, not three, lies. The statue is *not* of John Harvard, who was *not* the founder of Harvard University, which was *not* founded in 1638, and does *not* stand in Harvard Yard in front of University Hall. He sits.

While John Harvard's nonlegacy lives on, his original bequest of four hundred books, which got the school named after him, was destroyed in a fire in 1764. Only one book survived: *Christian Warfare against the Devil, World, and Flesh*. It's on display at the Houghton Library in Harvard Yard.

What You Get When You Cross Einstein with the Three Stooges
Cambridge

You have to hand it to those techno-minds at MIT: They sure know how to hack. Since the technical institute first opened in 1861, the brainy students have been pulling creative practical jokes that are both technically challenging and devilishly clever. Over the years the ever-more-ambitious hacks, as they are called, have become an institution.

Some pranks have been elegantly simple, like the stoplight altered to read "Don't Walk—Chew," instead of "Walk." Others were more scientifically challenging. In 1976, for example, hackers consulted an arachnologist and used an electron microscope to study spider webs before weaving a wicked-big one out of 1,250 feet of wire and rope and installing it in a campus building. The real trick, as with all hacks, was not to get snared by the police.

In 1982, during the Harvard–Yale football game, hackers hid a weather balloon inscribed with MIT under the turf of Harvard's 40-yard line. The pranksters inflated the balloon by remote control. The crowd and teams looked aghast as the balloon grew to 6 feet in diameter and exploded in a burst of white smoke. MIT 1, Harvard–Yale 0.

MIT's famed domes have long been favorite places for hackers to pull their pranks. One Halloween, hackers dressed the Great Dome in a 20-foot-tall witch's hat. Another year the huge dome was transformed into the *Star Wars* robot R2D2. The dome has been topped with a working telephone booth that rang when officials tried to remove it. Hackers also turned the pinnacle into a parking space for a full-size replica of a campus police car, complete with working lights, with a box of doughnuts on the front seat.

Hacks have to be harmless as well as humorous. Self-deprecating humor works well. In 1996 MIT student hackers transformed the Great Dome into a giant, working propeller beanie. Who says nerds have no sense of humor?

The 1982 weather balloon inflator that disrupted
the Harvard–Yale football game.

A Cemetery to Die For

Cambridge

There are almost as many people buried in Mount Auburn Cemetery in Cambridge (93,000 and counting) as there are living in the city (101,000). The historic cemetery is a popular place for very permanent residents and visitors alike. More than 200,000 people a year visit the burial grounds, making it one of Cambridge's most popular tourist destinations.

The Mount Auburn Cemetery Sphinx is only one of the reasons that make this a popular tourist destination.

Founded in 1831 by the Massachusetts Horticultural Society, Mount Auburn was the first landscaped cemetery in America. Its creation marked a dramatic change in the prevailing attitudes about death and burial, as it was designed not only to be a decent place of interment but also to serve as a cultural institution. Mount Auburn, unlike other early city cemeteries, utilized landscape architecture in its planning. This influenced the creation of no less than fifteen other park-cemeteries in the United States. Besides its obvious function, Mount Auburn serves as a museum, a sculpture garden, an arboretum, and a wildlife sanctuary.

Among the notables making the 175-acre garden their final residence are Oliver Wendell Holmes, Winslow Homer, Fanny Farmer, B. F. Skinner, and Buckminster Fuller.

The grave site of Mary Baker Eddy, founder of the Church of Christ, Scientist, is one of the more spectacular. Contrary to longstanding rumors, she did not have a telephone installed in her crypt. During the construction of her monument, Eddy's body was kept in the cemetery's receiving vault. A guard was hired to stay with the body until it was interred and the tomb was sealed. A telephone was installed at the receiving vault for the guard's use during that period. There was never a phone at Eddy's monument.

Mount Auburn Cemetery is open every day of the year from 8:00 a.m. to 5:00 p.m. During daylight saving time, hours are extended to 7:00 p.m. Drive-by and walking audio tours are available on tape for rent or purchase at the entrance gate or the office. The cemetery is located at 580 Mount Auburn Street, Cambridge. For additional information, call (617) 547-7105.

The Original Airhead and His Ignoble Ig Nobel Prizes
Cambridge

Marc Abrahams is an airhead and proud of it. In fact, as publisher of the *Annals of Improbable Research,* or *AIR,* Abrahams is head airhead. *AIR* is what would happen if the editors of *Mad* and the *National*

★ ★

Lampoon conspired to publish *Scientific American.* Lest you think being an airhead is somehow an ignoble distinction, the magazine has eight Nobel Prize laureates on its editorial board.

Since 1990 *AIR* has injected spoofs, parodies, and satires into the otherwise straitlaced world of science and scientists. Examples of typical articles include "Why the Chicken Must Come First," "Mass Strandings of Horseshoe Crabs," and an inquiry titled "What Does Crime Taste Like?" A regular feature queries Nobel Prize winners with the most pressing questions of our time, such as "Do you shave with a blade razor or electric?" and "Do you often give people nicknames?"

The highlight of the year for Abrahams and *AIR* is the annual Ig Nobel Prize ceremony, honoring people whose achievements "cannot or should not be reproduced." This takeoff on the Stockholm proceedings includes some of the pomp, along with a heavy dose of Swedish slapstick. Abrahams sports a tuxedo and top hat to announce the winners, including a biologist who studied how various flavors of chewing gum affect brain waves. Karl Kruszelnicki of the University of Sydney received his Ig Nobel Prize for his comprehensive survey of human belly button lint: who gets it, when, what color, and how much. Chris McManus of University College, London, was honored for his excruciatingly balanced report "Scrotal Asymmetry in Man and in Ancient Sculpture." A recent Ig Nobel in Medicine went to Brian Witcombe of Gloucester, England, and Dan Meyer of Antioch, Tennessee, for their penetrating study "Sword Swallowing and Its Side Effects." A Peace Prize went to the Air Force Research Laboratory in Dayton, Ohio, for instigating research and development on a chemical weapon—the so-called gay bomb—that will make enemy soldiers become sexually irresistible to each other.

Among other Ig winners: Purdue University professor George Goble received the 1996 prize in chemistry for dousing 60 pounds of charcoal with 3 gallons of liquid nitrogen, setting a world record for barbecue ignition, taking three seconds to turn the briquettes into ashes. Playing with fire was also a factor in the 1999 Ig Peace Prize. Charl

Fourie and Michelle Wong won for a flame-throwing, anti-car-jacking device. As the Good Book says, "Ashes to ashes."

The Ig ceremony, featuring opera, interpretive dance by Nobel laureates, and drama, takes place in Sanders Theatre at Harvard University the first week of October and is broadcast on National Public Radio's *Talk of the Nation: Science Friday,* the day after Thanksgiving. Check your local listings and be prepared to fall out of your seat.

Harvard's Hot Book
Cambridge

Early in the history of this country, men were men, women were women, and the religious were zealots. John Harvard was reared in these hellfire-and-brimstone days, taking his degrees from Emmanuel College, which was the Puritans' educational stomping grounds. The religious background left its mark. Eventually he married the sister of one of his classmates, who would eventually become the private secretary to Oliver Cromwell, and also came into money after his mother's death. Ultimately, he and his wife moved to the colonies, where they did quite well for themselves, and John became a teaching elder at the First Church of Charlestown.

Alas, he died early, at age thirty, and left more than 800 pounds to a new college that was established the year he was married. That school was later named after him by the General Court of Massachusetts Bay. But money is not the only thing he left. The bequest included his 400-volume library, virtually all of which went up in flames in a 1764 fire. According to tradition, the single volume left was the fourth edition of *The Christian Warfare against the Devil, World, and Flesh ... And Means to Obtain Victory,* by John Downame, published in 1634. A choice to make an evangelistic Bruce Willis proud.

As to whether the book belonged to Harvard and was the only one of his that had survived, there are questions and evidence. Inside the book's display case is a note dated May 24, 1843, from the college librarian at the time, who wrote, "This book is the only one

★ ★

in the Library which, beyond a doubt, was given by John Harvard."
There is some additional evidence: three numbers written inside the
front cover that would have placed the book as the eighth volume on
the second shelf of the third bookshelf. Furthermore, a 1723 library
catalog lists the title. Today you can see it in a display in the lobby of
Harvard's Houghton Library, along with copies of some of the other
books that were lost. The library is in Harvard Yard, facing Quincy
Street between the Lamont and Widener libraries.

One If by Land
Cambridge

Every year, millions of American grade schoolers must hear Longfellow's lines, "Listen, my children, and you shall hear of the midnight
ride of Paul Revere." Perhaps poetry, but not history. Ah, the power
of public relations codified in verse. Contrary to popular opinion, the

The midnight ride of, er, William Dawes
doesn't have the same ring to it as Revere.

famous silversmith was not the sole agent of warning. He and William Dawes, a tanner, took different routes to warn residents, and both eventually arrived in Lexington to alert Sam Adams and John Hancock. They ran into Samuel Prescott, out at 1:00 a.m. after seeing a local lady friend, and all three then headed to Concord. All three were stopped by the British in Lincoln. Revere was detained. Dawes, who had gotten by a patrol earlier in the evening by pretending to be drunk, escaped but fell off his horse and had to walk back to Lexington, only to return the next day to find the watch that had dropped from his pocket. Prescott, the unplanned accomplice, was the only one to reach the town where the patriots' arsenal was kept. You can see where one part of the ride occurred near the intersection of Massachusetts Avenue and Garden Street. A series of brass horseshoes set into the sidewalk are on the path that Dawes was thought to have taken through what is now Harvard Square. Supposedly, someone had his niece ride on her horse and measured the distance between hoofmarks so that the memorial to Dawes would be as accurate as possible. Clearly, Longfellow could have learned a thing or two about attention to details.

Guess Who's Writing about Dinner?

Cambridge

Ever have trouble deciding what to make for dinner? When in a mood like that, whatever you do, avoid the Schlesinger Library at the Radcliff Institute for Advanced Study. At a current 15,000 titles, its choice of culinary works may leave you with your mouth watering and yet further from a decision than ever before. The start of the collection was a group of books about cookery intended to document the "domestic focus and contributions of women," according to the Schlesinger's Web site. Someone should have added "industry" to the list. Since the humble beginnings, the collection has become appetite taking in scope, covering, among other things, the history of domestic life, culinary professions, culture, and gastronomy, with some

161

titles having their origins in the sixteenth century. There aren't just books, but magazines and microreproductions of manuscripts. Also in the collection are the papers of such culinary giants as writer M. F. K. Fisher; chef and television star Julia Child; Alice Bradley, editor of the magazine of the Boston Cooking School; Eleanor Lowenstein, proprietress of the Corner Book Shop, a New York bookstore that specialized in cookbooks; and Elizabeth David, who taught the British to embrace French and Italian cooking. The library is open to "anyone whose work requires the use of our collections," which is the literary equivalent of telling people to come in for a cup of coffee and a piece of pie. The Schlesinger is at 10 Garden Street; hours can be found at www.radcliffe.edu/schles/hours.aspx.

Tiptoe through the Tulips . . . Carefully
Cambridge

A New England urban area like Cambridge can feel dreary in the dead of winter as the snow turns to gray slush and the season feels as if it will go on for months. (And it will.) But for those near Harvard, there is visual relief in the form of the Glass Flowers collection at the Harvard Museum of Natural History. Over three thousand models representing more than 830 plant species were crafted by a father and son team, Leopold and Rudolph Blaschka, starting in 1886 and continuing for the next fifty years. Far from flat stained glass, the exhibits are sculpted out of hot glass, internally reinforced by thin wires, with painstakingly botanical accuracy. A Harvard professor, Lincoln Goodale, started the project because he wanted accurate models that would allow better teaching of botany.

They are stunning to behold, with rich colors that seem to pick up the display lights and enhance them. What makes them even more amazing is that they are all life-sized, making the amount of patience and care—as well as the eyesight—of the glassworkers remarkable. Now consider two other things that are as noteworthy. First, each flower over the five decades had to be packed and shipped from the

Blaschka studios near Dresden, Germany, to Harvard, a process that could take months, right up to World War II. Yet very few of the models broke on the way, a tribute to packing that was as determined as the craftsmanship. Second, the Blaschkas had to work from real samples of flowers, which meant that someone had to ship the plants, live, to their studios in the first place. You'll find that the trip to see the flowers is considerably less demanding.

While you're at the museum, you might want to see a few other curious things: a thirty-five-million-year-old bee; the world's largest frog; and the only known kronosaurus, a 42-foot-long prehistoric marine reptile. A pair of George Washington's pheasants reside in a glass corner case, a gift to the founding father from the Marquis de Lafayette. When the pheasants died, a taxidermist had them stuffed and mounted. The birds must have overheard a foul- (or is it fowl?) mouthed visitor, because they were recently put on indefinite loan to a museum in Philadelphia.

Go to 26 Oxford Street, just past Harvard Yard. Hours and other information are available at www.hmnh.harvard.edu.

The Russian Belle Bells
Cambridge

Usually, when you hear stories of institutions returning priceless artworks of another country, you can bet on a dubious acquisition process finally righted. But in the case of the Russian bells at Harvard, the exchange of an old set for a new one was a story of rescue and preservation. By 1922 bell ringing had been banned in Russia, and authorities had started to strip bells from their towers and melt them down. In 1929 Josef Stalin had increased the pace at which he was destroying any physical remnants of Russian spiritual practices. That was the year officials took a set of eighteen bells from the Danilov Monastery, a building near Moscow that was constructed in the thirteenth century. Intended, as so many others, to be turned into scrap, the 25-ton set was saved by Charles R. Crane, onetime American ambassador to

★ ★

Keeping a Lid on History

They say that if you don't learn from history, you're doomed to repeat it. But what if you can't get at it? Back in 1939, MIT was putting a cyclotron into place for nuclear research. Someone had the bright idea of burying a time capsule, which can offer an interesting link to the past. And so the engineers and scientists did, placing a brass container under a giant magnet, intending that the capsule would be unearthed fifty years later. Five decades passed, and everyone had forgotten that the capsule even existed. Eventually someone's synapses started firing, and people realized that there was a bit of history waiting to be reclaimed. There was just one problem: Although the cyclotron had long since been decommissioned, the equipment was still in place, including the 18-ton magnet under which the capsule lay. Oops.

China, heir to a Chicago industrialist, and one of the original financers of oil exploration in Saudi Arabia and Yemen. He acquired the bells and eventually brought them out of Russia and donated them to Harvard, where they were placed in various buildings. A lucky thing, because the bronze set became among the few examples to survive the cultural purges.

Eventually the Berlin Wall came down, communism ended in Russia, and conditions changed. Starting in 2007, Harvard began to ship the bells back to their original home. A new set, cast by the Vera Foundry in Voronezh, Russia, which is reviving the art of casting bells, arrived to take the place of their elder cousins. They hang at the Baker Library at the Harvard Business School and in the tower of Lowell House, an undergraduate dormitory. To this day, the Lowell House Society of Russian Bell Ringers tolls their charges on Sunday afternoons from 1:00 to 1:30 p.m., and guests are invited to ring them. If you can't make it to 10 Holyoke Place, consider pointing a browser to www.danilovbells.com, where you can see images from Web cams trained on both sets of bells.

The Twilight Zone

Cambridge

Do you love science fiction? Not like. *Love.* If so, then there's a place you're going to love: the MIT Science Fiction Society, or MITSFS (sometimes mocked on campus as MISFITS). The group claims to have the world's largest open-shelf collection of science fiction. We're talking about a collection that reputedly includes over 90 percent of all science fiction ever published in English, and some in other languages. Unlike many campus-based organizations, membership to this one is open to anyone who is willing to pay the dues (including one option for a membership that would last the lifetime of the holder and another for an inheritable membership that is good while the group is in existence). There are meetings in the library on Friday evenings, though, before attending, you might want to read some of the back minutes on the site to get a sense of what the members are like. Don't say we didn't warn you. The MITSFS is on the fourth floor of the Student Center at 84 Massachusetts Avenue. You can find those all-important meeting minutes as well as an online catalog of the books they have by visiting www.mit.edu/~mitsfs.

MIThenge

Cambridge

If you want to see how an artificial edifice reacts to celestial events, you don't need to head to Stonehenge in England. A trip at the right time of year to 77 Massachusetts Avenue should do the trick. That's one end of MIT's "Infinite Corridor," a hallway that runs through many of the oldest classroom buildings on campus. It's a landmark on the campus, with a lobby in the middle that opens out into a large courtyard in front of the large dome. In that stretch you can find bake sales, ticket booths for theatrical productions, and students rushing to class. Twice a year, though, for a two- to four-day window in November and January, there is a special occurrence when the position of the sun causes it to shine down the length of the corridor. The entire floor lights up in an orange glow. Clearly, you should not look directly into the sun, but otherwise it's a participant sport that requires no special preparation or capability—you don't even need Druid costumes. Just make sure that the day is clear before you take up your post. Shortly before zero hour, you want to walk the length of the corridor to reach the end farthest from Massachusetts Avenue and then head to the third floor in Building 8, which is the one at the end of the corridor. The time the event occurs is generally between 4:00 and 5:00 p.m.

A group on campus has calculated the days and times of MIThenge through January 2100; you can find the data at http://web.mit.edu/mithenge/mithenge-data.text.

Where's the Moat?
Cambridge

On 44 Bow Street, there is as odd a building as you will find near Harvard Square, a mock Flemish castle with a purple-and-yellow door that opens into one of the more secretive and slapstick parts of Harvard University that you might find: the Harvard Lampoon Castle. It is home to the *Harvard Lampoon,* a humor publication whose length of existence on campus is only trumped by that of the *Harvard Crimson.* But, hey, the laugh is on them, because the *Lampoon* has managed to become the longest-running, continuously published English-language humor magazine that is still in production. The *Lampoon* styled itself after *Punch,* eventually licensed its name to the *National Lampoon* (creating an admirable and significant revenue flow to the organization), and has been the generator of significant talent in writing and performance, including Conan O'Brien (host of *The Tonight Show*), George Plimpton (cofounder of *The Paris Review*), Fred Gwynne (actor who appeared, among other roles, as Herman Munster in *The Munsters*), John Updike (author of the *Rabbit* series), William Randolph Hearst (publishing magnate), George Santayana (philosopher and writer), and Robert Benchley (writer for *The New Yorker*). It's tough to get into the front door and even tougher to join the reputedly wild parties.

Harvard's historic Lampoon House.

Clang, Clang, Clang Went the T Stop

Cambridge

In and around Boston, the subway is called the T. But the only station you'll find that has mechanical human-powered instruments is the Kendall Square station on the Red Line. Travelers on the platform waiting for a train can pull a series of levers that attach via wires to mallets, which, in turn, hit pieces of metal. It's a cross between musical instrument, art, and physics experiment designed by Paul Matisse, grandson of Henri Matisse and a Harvard grad. Back in the mid-1980s, he was asked to design something that would help beautify the station. The result has been chiming … uh, charming people ever since. Not that the collection, called the Kendall Square Band, is always cooperative. Many often overestimate how much force is needed to move the levers. As a result, the wires break, and at times the instruments can stand mute. If you don't mind the chance of having the setup string you along, head to the Kendall Square T station and look for the levers.

Dead Pet in Dedham

Dedham

Founded in 1907, the Pine Ridge Cemetery for Small Animals is the oldest continuously operated pet cemetery in the country. It's run by the Animal Rescue League of Boston. The bucolic twenty-eight-acre site is the final resting place for over ten thousand animals, including many celebrity pets. Among the notables are horses from the Boston police department's mounted unit and murderess Lizzie Borden's beloved bowsers, Donald Stuart, Royal Nelson, and Laddie Miller. Oddly, Borden's dogs' tombstone is an exact replica of the one belonging to her parents in Fall River, Massachusetts. Polar explorer Richard Byrd's terrier, Igloo, is also buried in the cemetery. A pinkish stone chiseled in the shape of an iceberg with a carved inscription marks the spot. Byrd's faithful companion accompanied him on expeditions to both the Arctic and Antarctic. For information, contact the Pine Ridge Animal Center, 238 Pine Street; (781) 326-0729.

Black Dahlia Monument
Medford

One of the stranger monuments in Massachusetts was designed and paid for by the documentary filmmaker Kyle J. Wood, whose film *Medford Girl* chronicles the life and death of Elizabeth Short, the "Black Dahlia." Short was born in Hyde Park, Massachusetts, in 1924 and grew up in Medford. She quit school at age sixteen, seeking fame and fortune in Hollywood. Her mutilated body, severed in half at the waist, was found in a vacant lot in Hollywood in 1947—one of the most celebrated unsolved mysteries of its time. In 2006 director Brian De Palma made a feature film about the case.

The Black Dahlia monument is located at 115 Salem Street.

The Black Dahlia's memorial.

★ ★

Jumbo in a Jar
Medford

Although students at Tufts University are called Jumbos, it's not that they are especially big. They hold that nickname because the school's original mascot was P. T. Barnum's famous elephant, Jumbo. Born in Africa in 1859, Jumbo grew to 12 feet high at the shoulder and weighed more than 6 tons. Barnum, ever the showman, billed the

A jar of crunchy Peter Pan peanut butter is the
final resting place of Jumbo, the elephant.

huge pachyderm as the largest land animal ever in captivity. Big as he was, today all that remains of Jumbo are some ashes stored in a 14-ounce Peter Pan peanut butter jar locked in the safe of the school's athletic director.

The story of how Jumbo went from circus center ring to a crunchy peanut butter jar at college begins in 1882, when Barnum bought Jumbo from the London Zoo for $10,000. Jumbo traveled the circus circuit in a specially built railroad car until 1885, when he was hit by a train and died. The pachyderm underwent taxidermy, and the stuffed hide was taken on a four-year world tour. Jumbo then came to his final resting place at the Barnum Museum at Tufts University, where the ringmaster was a school trustee. Jumbo stood there for eighty-six years, while generations of students stuffed his trunk with pennies and pulled his tail for good luck on tests. In 1942 Jumbo underwent an overhaul, and his original overtugged tail was archived at the school's library.

All was well until 1975, when a fire destroyed the Barnum building, turning everything, including the elephant, into a pile of ashes. Mindful of the mascot's importance to Tufts, a member of the school's athletic department scooped up what he assumed were Jumbo's ashes and put them into the container he had on hand—an empty peanut butter jar—which is now kept in a safe in the athletic director's office. To this day Tufts Jumbos rub the jar for luck just before a big game. The tail on Jumbo's tush is in Tufts' Tisch Library Digital Collections and Archives. Say that three times fast and win a Kewpie doll.

Elephant Man Has a Herd Instinct

Medford

It's probably a good thing that John Baronian did not attend the University of California–Santa Cruz or Cal State–Long Beach. Otherwise, you might be reading about the world's largest collection of banana slugs or dirtbags. Baronian, you see, collected miniature models of his

✦ ✦

alma mater's mascot. As luck would have it, he went to Tufts University, home of Jumbo, the elephant, and so for fifty years Baronian collected elephant figurines.

Baronian began gathering his mini-menagerie of mini *objets de pachyderm* soon after graduation. He donated the bulk of the collection of some four thousand figurines—the largest assemblage of pachyderm art on the planet—to his alma mater. (If you've heard of a bigger herd, let us know.) The collection includes elephants made out of wood, glass,

"Mr. Tufts," John Baronian, with members
of his mini-elephant menagerie.

★ ★

bronze, porcelain, and, yes, ivory. There are elephant ashtrays, mugs, jewelry, and bookends and a pachyderm jigsaw puzzle.

Baronian passed away in 2008, but the school won't soon forget the man they call "Mr. Tufts." John Baronian was a man with a big heart and a herd to match. For many years he served as a jumbo Jumbo supporter, volunteering his services as a fund raiser and generously donating money to the university. The Baronian Herd now resides in the Remis Sculpture Court at the Aidekman Arts Center, 40R Talbot Avenue, on Tufts' Medford campus. Call ahead for hours at (617) 627-3518.

This Sign Will "Sleigh" You
Medford

We hate dashing your Christmas spirit, but one of the most popular songs sung around the holiday has nothing to do with Christmas. "Jingle Bells" was written by Medford resident James Pierpont in 1850, inspired by the annual one-horse open-sleigh races on Salem and Pleasant Streets between Medford Square and Malden Square. Pierpont penned the racy little ditty in Simpson's Tavern, a boardinghouse that had the only piano in town. The lyrics tell the story of picking up girls while hot-rodding through the snow.

The song was originally titled "One Horse Open Sleigh," and initially it was a flop. But after a Boston publishing house released it as "Jingle Bells" in 1859, the rest was history, albeit controversial history. It seems that Savannah, Georgia, thinks it's the "'Jingle Bells' capital of the world" because Pierpont was living there when the song was released and is also buried there. However, a plaque at 21 High Street near the corner of Forest Street in Medford sets things right. As residents in Medford are quick to point out, Pierpont wrote the tune while in Massachusetts . . . and racing a sleigh in snowless Savannah doesn't make much sense, anyway. (In fairness to Savannah, it too has a plaque commemorating the composer of "Jingle Bells.")

Medford is also where the lyrics for another famous festive song were written. Town resident Lydia Maria Child's poem "Boy's

Thanksgiving" became the song "Over the River and Through the Woods." Child lived in the Greek Revival house at 114 Ashland Street on the corner of Salem Street, not far from where Pierpont "sleighed" them with "Jingle Bells." Behind Child's house are the woods she went through and the Mystic River over which she traveled to get to Grandfather's house. We're told the horse knows the way.

Marathon Man

Newton

John Kelley liked to run and run and run. Between 1928 and 1992, John "the Elder" Kelley, a Massachusetts native, ran the Boston Marathon sixty-one times, finishing all but three races. He came in first in two races (1935 and 1945), took second place a record seven times,

At the foot of Heartbreak Hill is the monument to Boston Marathon man John Kelley.

and finished in the top ten eighteen times. He was also an Olympian (1936 and 1948).

Kelley ran his last marathon when he was eighty-five and became the first road runner elected to the National Track and Field Hall of Fame. Officials waived the retirement rule because they figured he might never retire. Kelley died on October 6, 2004, at the age of ninety-seven. He was selected "Runner of the Century" by *Runner's World* magazine.

A statue dedicated to the amazing marathoner as a young man and as an older participant is located at Heartbreak Hill, on the corner of Walnut Street and Commonwealth Avenue in Newton, across from City Hall.

In the 1996 centennial running of the Boston Marathon, 39,708 official entrants participated in the race. According to the *Guinness World Records,* this is the largest number of runners in a single race in history.

Art Too Bad to Be Ignored
Somerville

The Museum of Bad Art (MOBA) is testimony to the wisdom of writer Marshall McLuhan, who said, "Art is anything you can get away with." The museum is dedicated to "the collection, preservation, exhibition, and celebration of bad art in all its forms and all its glory." In short, it's a permanent repository for art too bad to be ignored.

What started out in 1995 in a suburban basement as a humble assemblage of spectacularly awful artwork has evolved into a full-fledged museum, complete with the requisite gift shop. The MOBA holds a special place near and dear to connoisseurs of misunderstood masterpieces. It's also located within earshot of the men's room at the Dedham Community Theater. The world seems awash with art that stinks. Recently, MOBA expanded to the basement of the Somerville Theater in Davis Square.

To qualify for an esteemed place in the museum's collection, an artist should display ambition that vastly exceeds his or her ability. One classic museum piece, for example, portrays a naked woman in

stiletto heels and red leg warmers sitting on a stool milking a unicorn. The unicorn looks startled but not displeased by the experience. It's truly a head-snapping, jaw-dropping sight.

MOBA curators are constantly searching Salvation Army stores and landfills in search of the highest-caliber bad art. The majority of the collection came from bequests of the public refuse system. Submissions are always welcome. The curators have imposed a $6.50 limit on acquiring new works but once offered twice that amount as a reward for a piece that was stolen. (Alas, even at that price the painting was never recovered.)

MOBA's permanent gallery is in the basement of the Dedham Community Theater, 580 High Street in Dedham Center and at Somerville Theater, 55 Davis Square, Somerville. Admission is free with the price of a movie ticket. For some really great bad art, visit the Web site: www.museumofbadart.org.

What the Fluff

Somerville

Sure, Somerville is the birthplace of Bette Davis, and it's where the first telephone wire was installed, but the city's real claim to fame is for what resident Archibald Query concocted in 1917: Fluff. You know the marshmallow spread that forms the backbone of the fluffernutter sandwich?

Query whipped up the first batch of the goo in his basement kitchen on Springfield Street just off Union Square. He sold the recipe three years later to H. Allen Durkee and Fred L. Mower, whose company continues to crank out the stuff in their Salem, Massachusetts, factory.

In 2006 then state senator Jarrett Barrios raised a flap over Fluff when he proposed an amendment to a junk food bill that would have limited the serving of the white stuff in schools. A representative from Somerville countered the proposal with a suggestion to name the fluffernutter as the official state sandwich.

Nothin' came of the idea, but on the last Saturday in September residents of Somerville pay homage to Query's contribution to tooth

What the Fluff!

decay and celebrate WTF (What the Fluff) day. There's a cooking contest for the most creative Fluff dessert recipe, a fluffernutter eating contest, and dance routines featuring the Fluffettes.

Feelings
Watertown

Most museums have signs up asking you not to touch the exhibits. The Perkins Museum is the complete opposite. Located at the Perkins School for the Blind, famous in part as the place where Helen Keller eventually came to study, the museum tells the story of the school and the many developments in educating students who are blind or deaf-blind in subjects including music, math, reading, writing, geography, science, and sports. So allowing people to touch exhibits takes on a new meaning. Perhaps the most unusual item in the museum is the largest and oldest tactile globe in the United States. If you'd like to expand your concept of a world of the senses, the museum is open Tuesday and Thursday from 2:00 to 4:00 p.m. Go to 175 North Beacon Street and head to the Howe Building. For more information, point a browser to http://perkins.pvt.k12.ma.us/museum/.

Art Imitates Death
Watertown

Part of the permanent collection at the Armenian Library and Museum of America in Watertown, Massachusetts, are pictures painted by Dr. Jack Kevorkian. Known to many as "Doctor Death," Kevorkian is a controversial physician who promotes assisted suicide and was imprisoned for eight years for practicing what he preaches. He was convicted of second-degree murder in 1999 for giving a lethal injection to a fifty-two-year-old man with Lou Gehrig's disease. Kevorkian is also an oil painter of some note, and being an ethnic Armenian, he has donated a number of his works to the Armenian Library and Museum. Two of his oils, *A Very Still Life* and *Genocide,* are hanging in the museum at 65 Main Street, Watertown. For more information, call (617) 926-2562.

Art imitates death.

index

index

index

index

about the authors

Bruce Gellerman hosts Public Radio International's environmental program *Living on Earth* and is founder of SoundTreks LLC, which creates location-aware content for the mobile media market.

Bruce was a science reporter for NPR and senior Washington correspondent for the Center for Investigative Journalism. His work has appeared in the *New York Times* and the *Boston Globe,* as well as on BBC Radio and *60 Minutes.* He has received more than forty national awards for journalism. Bruce lives in Watertown, Massachusetts, with his wife, Yulia, and their children, Andre and Anya.

Journalist Erik Sherman's writing and photographs have appeared in many national publications, including *Newsweek,* the *New York Times Magazine,* the *Financial Times,* and *Continental.* He is also the author of *The Complete Idiot's Guide to Pizza and Panini, The Complete Idiot's Guide to Cannon EOS Digital Cameras,* and *Everything Leadership.*

Bruce and Erik are the co-authors of *Massachusetts Curiosities.*